THE GREAT EMU WAR

by Xavier Coy

ORiGiN™
Theatrical

FOR ALL ENQUIRIES CONTACT: ORiGiN™ Theatrical
PO BOX Q1235, QVB Post Office, Sydney, NSW, 1230, Australia
Phone: (61 2) 8514 5201
enquiries@originmusic.com.au   www.origintheatrical.com.au
Part of the ORiGiN™ Music Group
An Australian Independent Music Company

IMPORTANT NOTICE

First Published © 2024 ORiGiN™ Theatrical

The amateur and professional acting rights to this work are controlled exclusively by ORiGiN™ Theatrical (the publisher). Permission in writing is required by ORiGiN™ Theatrical, or their agent, before a performance is given. A performance is given any time it is acted before an audience. A royalty fee is payable before each and every performance regardless of whether it is for a non-profit organisation or if an admission is charged.

The publication of this play does not mean that the amateur and professional performance rights are available. It is highly recommended that you apply for performance rights before starting rehearsals and/or booking rehearsal or performance spaces.

Visit the ORiGiN™ Theatrical website for applications and information www.origintheatrical.com.au or address your inquiry to ORiGiN™ Theatrical, PO Box Q1235, QVB Post Office, Sydney, NSW 1230, Australia.

This work is fully protected by copyright. No alterations, substitutions or deletions can be made to this work without the prior consent of the publisher. It is expressly prohibited to broadcast, televise, film, videotape, record, translate or transmit to subscribers through a diffusion service that currently exists or is yet to be invented, this work or any portion thereof whatsoever without permission in writing from the publisher.

Copying or reproducing, without permission, of all or any part of this book, in any form, is an infringement of copyright. Copyright provides the creators with an incentive to invest their time, talent and other resources to create new works. Authors earn their living from the royalties they receive from book sales and from the performance of the work. Copyright law provides a legal framework for control of their creations.

Whenever this play is produced, the billing and credit requirements *must* appear on all programs distributed in connection with the performance and in all instances in which the title of the play appears for the purposes of advertising, seeking publicity for the play or otherwise exploiting the play and/or a performance(s).

While this play may contain references to brand names or trademarks owned by third parties, or make reference to public figures, ORiGiN™ Theatrical should not be considered to be necessarily endorsing or otherwise attempting to promote an affiliation with any of the owners of the brand names or trademarks or public figures. Such references are solely for use in a dramatic context.

LANGUAGE NOTE

Licensees are welcome to make small alterations to the language that is used is this play so as to make it suitable for a younger cast and/or audience.

MUSIC USE NOTE

Licensees are solely responsible for obtaining formal written permission from copyright owners to use copyrighted music in the performance of this play and are strongly cautioned to do so. If no such permission is obtained by the licensee, then the licensee must use only original music that the licensee owns and controls. Licensees are solely responsible and liable for all music clearances and shall indemnify the copyright owners of the play(s) and their licensing agent, ORiGiN™ Theatrical, against any costs, expenses, losses and liabilities arising from the use of music by licensees. Please contact the appropriate music licensing authority in your territory for the rights to any incidental music. In Australia and New Zealand, contact APRA AMCOS apraamcos.com.au.

If you are in any doubt about any of the above then contact ORiGiN™ Theatrical.

For complete listing of plays and musicals available to perform and all licence enquiries, contact ORiGiN™ Theatrical.

---

www.origintheatrical.com.au
+ 61 2 8514 5201

AND HERE ARE THE RULES IN PLAIN ENGLISH FOR YOU...

DO NOT perform this play without getting permission from ORiGiN™ Theatrical first. In 99% of cases you'll need to pay us money to be allowed to stage a performance. This money goes to the author(s) of the show who shed blood, sweat and tears creating this play. Please don't rob them of their livelihood.
Go online www.origintheatrical.com.au or call +61 2 8514 5201

DO NOT make a copy of this book by photocopying, scanning, taking a photo, retyping (on a computer or a typewriter), or using a pencil, pen or chalkboard. If you want to purchase more copies contact ORiGiN™ Theatrical.
Go online www.origintheatrical.com.au or call +61 2 8514 5201

DO NOT make any changes to the text without first getting permission from ORiGiN™ Theatrical in writing. Sometimes you'll be allowed to make changes and sometimes you won't. Please always check with us first.
Go online www.origintheatrical.com.au or call +61 2 8514 5201

DO NOT record your performances or rehearsals in any way without first getting permission from ORiGiN™ Theatrical. We know everyone wants to try and record everything on their phones these days. We get it. But please don't encourage them or give them permission. Sometimes there are important contractual reasons as to why we can't give you permission to record it. And sometimes there aren't any reasons and we can say YES. Please just check with us first.
Go online www.origintheatrical.com.au or call +61 2 8514 5201

DO contact ORiGiN™ Theatrical if you have any questions about anything. At all. And we mean anything. One of us that works here (not me) has a peculiar interest in recording the unusual bird calls of the adult hoatzin (a species of tropical bird found in wet forest and mangrove of the Amazon and the Orinoco delta in South America) so we should be able to answer any questions you have about the Hoatzin. Plus we know some things about some other things too.

Thank you for taking the time to read this.

AUTHORS NOTE

Based on, perhaps the most ridiculous story in Australian history, The Great Emu War is ripe for satire. When I read about the true story of The Royal Australian Artillery being sent out to WA to wage war on an animal that is on our coat of arms I couldn't believe what I was reading. Not only did it seem like an insane waste of resources but it spoke to a deeper issue that we are facing in the world right now, climate change. For me this story was about Man vs Nature. There is no way for the people who populate the planet to overcome the might of Mother Nature.
I wanted to give a voice to the animals. We, of course, have intruded on their natural habitat and had the arrogance to believe that we can destroy anything to get what we want.
The Great Emu War is a satire of many elements of Australian society. I wanted to explore, among many things, the fragility of the male ego and masculinity and our relationship with alcohol. On a global level I wanted to satirize the frivolous attitude we have when it comes time to go to war.

CHARACTERS

Billy Westlake (M, 40's)
Major G.P.W. Meredith (M, 50's)
Clementine Westlake/Kerry-Anne (W, 40's)
Private Douglas Brown/Ron (M, 30)
Private Neville Kelly/Don (M, 20's)
Colonel Warwick Katter/Steve (M, 40's)
Reginald/Regina Turner/Priscilla (W, 20's)

Based on a true story...

AT RISE:

PROLOGUE:

Out of the darkness a soldier appears. We come to learn that this is BILLY WESTLAKE (40's, but at this time in his 20's). The soldier is holding a rifle, shaking, full of fear.

A bomb goes off next to him - a plume of smoke billows into the air - Billy screams out in fear.

He continues forward - his rifle at the ready - pointed straight towards the audience. His arms are quivering.

Another bomb goes off - this time the other side of him and closer - he jumps out of the way - another plume of smoke billows into the air.

        BILLY
Fuck, fuck, fuck.

Out of the darkness (in the audience) appears an enemy soldier.

        BILLY
Drop it. Drop it! Drop your weapon!

Billy is shaking.

            BILLY
I'm sorry.

            Billy shoots the gun as the lights crash to black.

ACT 1: THE WAR

SCENE 1 - PARLIAMENT

Major G.P.W. Meredith (50's) addresses Parliament, Sydney.

MAJOR MEREDITH

As has been the case throughout time - let me start again. Sorry, I - I thought I had this committed to memory. Mhmph.

Major Meredith pulls a piece of paper out of his pocket.

MAJOR MEREDITH

Ah yes. Sorry I just wanted to start off on the right- just pretend I didn't say that part before and I'll - our country has, for the few decades, endured some of the greatest adversity since...Well it's not really my place to, if we're talking historically, this country was colonized in a fairly disgusting - I shouldn't go off script. Anyway, back to - The Great War devastated this nation. We are now faced with a crisis seemingly as severe but not in terms of loss of life, rather income.

We have taken, what I believe to be, a wonderful step in supporting some of our returning servicemen. They have been afforded the opportunity to grow crops in parts of Western Australia we deem fit for farming with the hope that financial prosperity shall ensue. We have a duty to those that served to give back, to at all costs protect men. Our men - that's what I meant. Now, a new challenge awaits us.

Throughout history Man has always wrestled with the gallant

beast that is nature. Gallant as it may be, nature can be a cruel and ghastly demon. It stares us in the eye and batters us into submission, leaving a path of destruction in it's wake. Not all the time but sometimes, I didn't even write this fucking - sorry - fortunately Man has something that nature does not, brains. We have the ability to think, to outsmart. I put to you that we control nature, not the other way around.

When I was fighting in the Great War it wasn't wind that killed our men, it was bullets. Shot from a gun. By a person. Nature can't fire a gun. Mmm. Interesting, no?

I address you in parliament today to warn you of one of nature's new enemies to Man. The emu. In the noble pursuit of rewarding our soldiers who risked their lives for our nation we have been met with a rather pernicious beast who's interests seem to be solely in destroying the crops planted by our heroes. Make no mistake. This is war.

Standing erect at six feet and two inches and weighing up to fifty kilograms these flightless emblems of chaos are a scourge on society at large. We simply cannot sit idly by and let these long necked fucks run riot over this great nation of ours!

I apologize for my language thus far ladies and gentlemen, I um...I lose myself sometimes. Where was I...?

Ah yes! Today, I put to you here in Parliament, a motion to take back our Australia. To put nature back in it's box, to send the emu, our nation's worthless thief of honest labour's work, into oblivion and give our brave veterans a chance to live in prosperity and good health without the fear of feathery freaks decimating their crops and their livelihood. I ask Parliament for the assistance of the Royal Australian Artillery to take charge, to take back enemy lines and once again, make nature take a back seat. To make Australia great again. To make nature cower to the might of Man.

SCENE 2 - ARRIVAL AT WARRALAKIN

A small property in Warralakin, Western Australia. We're at the property of Billy (40's) and CLEMENTINE (30's) Westlake - it's the 1st of November, 1932. Scorching hot, unrelenting.

Billy - a veteran of WWI is now a wheat farmer. He's gruff and not particularly social although he will share a beer with any man.

Clementine - a suffragette stuck on a farm in rural Western Australia, unhappily. She's miles away from anyone. She is never far from a cigarette or a sherry (more likely beer).

Clementine is sitting on the deck with a cigarette in hand, reading a magazine, waiting for the soldiers to arrive.

On walk PRIVATE DOUGLAS BROWN (30) - handsome, sweet, a good soldier and his fellow soldier PRIVATE NEVILLE KELLY (20's) - nervous, prone to anxiety and a very poor soldier.

PRIVATE BROWN
Afternoon, madam.

CLEMENTINE
Christ, you're a looker.

PRIVATE BROWN
Thank you.

CLEMENTINE
Bet you get that all the time.

PRIVATE BROWN
Yes.

CLEMENTINE
Too pretty to be a soldier.

PRIVATE BROWN
Serving my nation, madam.

NEVILLE
Hello.

CLEMENTINE
Drop and dash, huh?

PRIVATE BROWN
Yes, well...It's a long drive back.

CLEMENTINE
They couldn't even pop in for a cup of tea.

PRIVATE BROWN
Unfortunately, no.

CLEMENTINE
There's always time for a cup of tea out here.

PRIVATE BROWN
I apologize on behalf of my fellow soldiers, madam.

CLEMENTINE
We haven't had visitors out here for three months. Three whole months and all I've had to talk to is Billy.
'I've had more beers today than you've had hot breakfasts.' 'I can run faster than a wombat.' 'Oh I think I've ruptured my testicle again.'
Couldn't even come in for a cup of tea.'

PRIVATE BROWN
He sounds like a fine man, your husband.

CLEMENTINE
What's your name?

PRIVATE BROWN
Private Douglas Brown, madam. At your service.

CLEMENTINE
Good shit. And you are?

NEVILLE
Neville.

Private Brown nudges him.

NEVILLE
Private Neville Kelly, ma'am. Proud member of the Royal Australian Artillery.

CLEMENTINE
Have you served?

NEVILLE
Um. No, ah - I'm on light duties generally because - well I like to think -

CLEMENTINE
My husband served in the War.

PRIVATE BROWN
Wonderful, madam. It's our honour to be here.

NEVILLE
Yes! An honour! It's a pleasure to be serving you and your husband who fought for our freedom. May the blood of our enemies be forever imprinted on his hands.

PRIVATE BROWN
Alright, Neville.

NEVILLE
Sorry that's -

CLEMENTINE
Changed him, the War.

PRIVATE BROWN
Yes, I've heard it does to some men.

CLEMENTINE
Before he left he was as dull as anything. All he'd drink was tea and water. The alcohol is ruining his brain but at least he's interesting now, I suppose.

NEVILLE
My friend from school became an alcoholic. He lives with his mother now. They have to keep him on a leash because he tried to bite the neighbour on the pecker.

PRIVATE BROWN
The pecker?

NEVILLE
Right square on the pecker.

CLEMENTINE
Your friend bit a man on his Johnson, Private?

NEVILLE
No ma'am, on the pecker.

PRIVATE BROWN
A Johnson's a pecker, Private.

NEVILLE
Good Lord. What do I mean?

PRIVATE BROWN
I couldn't tell you.

CLEMENTINE
Maybe he gnawed on his ging gang goolies.

NEVILLE
That's not - oh dear -

PRIVATE BROWN
It's okay, Private, madam is teasing you.

NEVILLE
Oh yes I know - I, I, I -

CLEMENTINE
People person, hey?

NEVILLE
No, madam, people find me unusual mostly.

CLEMENTINE
You're joking.

NEVILLE
I'm afraid I don't know how to, madam.

CLEMENTINE
That's quite a good one about the man biting the other man on the penis.

NEVILLE
His nose!

PRIVATE BROWN
His hooter?

NEVILLE
Hooter! Yes!

CLEMENTINE
Would you gentlemen like a beer?

PRIVATE BROWN
We probably shouldn't -

CLEMENTINE
Oh please you're not working today. You've had a long day's travel.

PRIVATE BROWN
Well, yes, a beer would be lovely in that case.

NEVILLE
Do you have any Sarsaparilla?

CLEMENTINE
It's beer, water or tea out here.

NEVILLE
A water would be lovely.

Clementine exits.

NEVILLE
I'm a ninny aren't I? I had everything planned out all in my head yesterday. I stood in front of the mirror and said 'Hello, madam, sir, my name is Private Neville Kelly. I'm here to be of service to you.'

Neville salutes.

NEVILLE
Did I salute? I didn't did I? Oh dear!

PRIVATE BROWN
You don't have to salute, Neville, you're fine.

NEVILLE
Darn it! I knew it! Everything went so fast I couldn't keep up. Did I make an idiot of myself?

PRIVATE BROWN
No, Neville, you're overthinking things.

NEVILLE
I have a habit of doing that, Douglas. When I was born the

doctor said he'd never seen a more worried baby. He said it looked like I tried to crawl back in. Sometimes I wish I did.

PRIVATE BROWN
It's a good thing you didn't, Neville, you know why? Aside from the deeply, deeply, scaring psychological trauma of being a baby rejected by Earth - you're here and I'm glad you're here.

NEVILLE
Really, Douglas?

PRIVATE BROWN
Of course I am, mate.

NEVILLE
That means a lot coming from you. You're the best looking person I've ever seen.

PRIVATE BROWN
Okay, that doesn't seem relevant, but thank you, Neville. You're a good man too.

NEVILLE
I can't stuff this up, Douglas.

PRIVATE BROWN
You won't.

NEVILLE
It's highly probable I will. Everything I've ever touched has turned to a rotten pile of poo-poo. My Dad was a Major. A

Major, Douglas. I can't even cook toast.

PRIVATE BROWN
I'm sure you've got other skills.

NEVILLE
Everywhere I go people say 'Oh you're Major Kelly's son aren't you? You must be a real top soldier.' And you know what I say to them? 'No, not me, I'm just his talentless spare dick son.'

PRIVATE BROWN
Spare dick's a bit rough, Neville.

NEVILLE
That's what father calls me. I even stuffed up my introduction.

PRIVATE BROWN
Okay, Neville, mate, you've gotta perk up a little. We just got here, you might do a fantastic job and then everyone will respect you.

NEVILLE
Maybe you're right, Douglas. Maybe this is the chance to redeem myself. They're only emus.

Billy appears.

BILLY
Only emus?

PRIVATE BROWN
Hello, sir, my name is -

BILLY
Did I hear you right, soldier?

PRIVATE BROWN
Private Kelly was just telling me about some of his insecurities -

BILLY
When I was in the War you know what I never did? Underestimate the enemy. There were some dark days out there. Sitting next to Frenchmen in fucken France. It was hell. I remember one day I was speaking to this French fucker his name was Jacques or some shit. We were a few hundred metres away from a German camp. He bet me a packet of darts that he could steal a frankfurter from the German's and be back without them even noticing. A frankfurter. We shook on it. He ran, snuck into the base, stole a handful of frankfurters and returned. Three days later he died of botulism, bacteria did him in. Do you know why I'm telling you this?

PRIVATE BROWN
Not really.

BILLY
Never underestimate the enemy.

Beat.

NEVILLE
Shouldn't we just be careful about eating certain meats?

BILLY
I've seen an emu kick the head of a dog straight off.

NEVILLE
Okay.

BILLY
You wanna be a dog?

NEVILLE
No.

BILLY
Bark.

NEVILLE
What?

BILLY
Bark. Do you think I'm joking?

PRIVATE BROWN
I think you should bark.

NEVILLE
Woof.

BILLY
That's right. That's right.

Clementine returns with beer.

CLEMENTINE
Oh good you've all met. I'm assuming you told them about the dog?

BILLY
Ken oath, I did.

CLEMENTINE
My husband's a barrel of laughs. What till the sun goes down and he gets stuck into the rusty water.

BILLY
Oi. You mean beer. Beer.

CLEMENTINE
They're not going to steal your whisky.

BILLY
You better not go near my giggle juice.

Clementine hands Neville his water.

BILLY
Where's your beer?

NEVILLE
Oh, um, alcohol tends to make me anxious.

BILLY
What the fuck? We're getting swarmed with emus and the best they send us is a bloke who gets nervous drinking a ten ounce sambo. Christ. Say goodbye to the crops, honey.

CLEMENTINE
Sorry, my husband's being a prick.

PRIVATE BROWN
We understand the concerns.

NEVILLE
No, I - I'm a good soldier - I'll um - you know, kill the bastards.

BILLY
You bloody better. Have a beer.

NEVILLE
Perhaps after my water.

BILLY
Have. A. Beeya.

Billy forces a beer into Neville's hand.

NEVILLE
Oh okay.

BILLY
Sip.

Neville has a tentative sip.

NEVILLE
Uh-huh. Yum. That's - thank you.

BILLY
Sip.

Neville sips again.

BILLY
Sip.

Neville sips once more.

CLEMENTINE
That's enough.

BILLY
You guys like a wrestle?

NEVILLE
I'm more of an observer than a participator.

CLEMENTINE
Christ this again.

BILLY
What? It's just a little wrestle.

CLEMENTINE
Go wrestle a cow if you're so desperate to handle some meat.

BILLY
Cows are shit wrestlers I've told you that a thousand times.

CLEMENTINE
Maybe the fact you've told me that a thousand times suggests you should stop asking everyone and everything you come into contact with to wrestle.

BILLY
There's nothing wrong with a bit of rough skin on skin, love. It's good for the soul. Come on, you.

NEVILLE
I've actually got a bit of eczema -

BILLY
Rank. Probably a good thing. I'd turn you into mince meat. What's this one's name? He looks like a goer.

CLEMENTINE
Dougal.

PRIVATE BROWN
Douglas actually -

BILLY
Alright Dougal top off, dacks down -

PRIVATE BROWN
I really don't think -

NEVILLE
Yes, Douglas! Wrestle the man!

BILLY
Yeah come on, Dougal! Come on! Come on. Come on. Have a dig ya dog.

CLEMENTINE
He'll keep going.

PRIVATE BROWN
Alright.

Billy whips off his shirt - he is ready to rock and roll. Douglas, meanwhile, is taking a little lugubrious... He takes off his shirt and whooshka! He is pinned to the floor.

BILLY
Give up?

PRIVATE BROWN
Yes.

BILLY
Say I'm Beta.

PRIVATE BROWN
What?

BILLY
Say I'm a little Beta male.

PRIVATE BROWN
I'm a little Beta male.

Billy releases his grasp. He high fives Neville.

NEVILLE
Nice work! You got smashed.

BILLY
Still got it.

CLEMENTINE
Well this has been fun hasn't it? Couple of men having a wrestle apropos of nothing. What a way to spend a Sunday.

BILLY
I had an old rugby mate Roger come stay with us a while back. After the games we'd hit the showers and someone'd yell out 'EXTRA TIME' and you'd drop your towels and lay into each other. Good clean fun. Anyway Roger came out to stay with us a while back -

CLEMENTINE
Roger was fun.

BILLY
We locked eyes, beers down and latched on. Dislocated his elbow. He was screaming. Little pansy. Drink up you wet sock, I've already had four.

PRIVATE BROWN
We shouldn't have too many, it's a big day tomorrow.

BILLY
You can't fight with a bit of a dusty nogan? What is this generation? You make me physically sick.

Billy leaves.

NEVILLE
I didn't catch his name.

CLEMENTINE
That's Billy. We got married before he went to War. I kind of assumed that he'd be killed over there...But it wasn't to be.

NEVILLE
I'm sorry to hear.

CLEMENTINE
Plans are useless. Look at me. I spend my days pulling on cow's udders, kicking dirt where the wheat crops should be, counting down the hours till I can go back to sleep, one more sleep till I inevitably close my eyes and die. At least I'm not living in Perth.

PRIVATE BROWN
Madam, I swear to you, here and now, that we will win this war. It's our duty to help you prosper and we will.

CLEMENTINE
You handsome idiot.

NEVILLE
You are very handsome.

CLEMENTINE
What makes you think you can overcome nature?

PRIVATE BROWN
We're armed with the finest in modern machinery. The Royal Australian Artillery have entrusted us with Lewis Guns, madam.

NEVILLE
They're big guns with lots of bullets that keep firing like duf duf duf -

CLEMENTINE
I know what a Lewis Gun is.

PRIVATE BROWN
Major George Meredith has entrusted us with five thousand rounds of ammunition. With all due respect to the emu - they are flightless and although they're fast, they cannot outrun a bullet.

CLEMENTINE
I hope you're right.

NEVILLE
Same here. I need this.

CLEMENTINE
I should get back. These cows aren't going to milk themselves. Make yourselves comfortable. I think you'll be here a while.

PRIVATE BROWN
Thank you, madam.

CLEMENTINE
Clementine.

Clementine leaves.

NEVILLE
I like her.

SCENE 3 - MARRIAGE

That night. Clementine and Billy are getting ready for bed. Billy, by now, is very drunk.

BILLY
Thought I saw a raindrop this arvo.

CLEMENTINE
Oh? About time. The land's as dry as a nun's -

BILLY
Just dribbled on meself.

CLEMENTINE
Brilliant.

BILLY
I nearly got one today, Clem.

CLEMENTINE
You say that every day.

BILLY
We stood there toe to toe. I ripped my shirt off, I said come on you dirty bird...And it ran off. Coward!

CLEMENTINE
How many times have I told you that you can't kill an emu with your bare hands, Billy.

BILLY
Fucken hogwash! Besides I've got a better chance than the deadshits they send us. That nervy looking prick looks like if he bought a kangaroo it wouldn't hop.

CLEMENTINE
Well it's better than nothing isn't it?

BILLY
And what's all that about not wanting a tinnie? I almost told him to hit the frog and toad then and there.

CLEMENTINE
Not everyone likes to drink, Billy.

BILLY
Yeah well that's ridiculous. You come to my house you have a brew. You don't want one you can piss off. You wanna have a root?

CLEMENTINE
Couldn't think of anything worse.

BILLY
Oh come on love.

CLEMENTINE
Are you off your fucken head?

BILLY
Well...Yeah.

CLEMENTINE
What makes you think I'd wanna have a roll around with you now?

BILLY
I'm a bit of alright.

CLEMENTINE
Look at yourself.

BILLY
Yeah I'm rugged.

CLEMENTINE
You're hammered.

BILLY
Look I know I'm no Clark Gable but there's something about me don't you reckon? Something a bit...Indescribable.

CLEMENTINE
Yeah I definitely can't describe it.

BILLY
Oh, Clem -

CLEMENTINE
Touch me and I'll knock your block off.

BILLY
Righto, righto. Do you still love me but? I love you my little chicken.

CLEMENTINE
Oh, God.

BILLY
I do!

CLEMENTINE
Shut up, Bill.

BILLY
What - you don't love me?

CLEMENTINE
You'll wake up the men.

BILLY
When I was in France -

CLEMENTINE
Not the French shit again.

BILLY
All that kept me from going insane was the thought of my little Clementine.

CLEMENTINE
And so when you got back you thought it was a great way to show me that by moving us to buttfucknowhere.

BILLY
Look, it may not be the ideal destination but it's home!

CLEMENTINE
This isn't home, Billy. This is a bar-ran wasteland.

BILLY
Well...How's this - once these bloody emu's are knocked off and we've got wheat money we'll move back to civilization.

CLEMENTINE
Yeah?

BILLY
Swear on mother.

CLEMENTINE
You hate your mother.

BILLY
Yeah that's why I'm swearing on her.

CLEMENTINE
You've gotta swear on something you like otherwise the oath is redundant.

BILLY
What'd you call me?

CLEMENTINE
It means null and void.

BILLY
Alright then if we get wheat money then we'll be nullenvoid.

CLEMENTINE
Great.

BILLY
Hey, Clem. I promise.

CLEMENTINE
Yep. You better. Cause I don't know much longer I can stand it here.

Billy makes his way towards the door.

CLEMENTINE
Where are you going?

BILLY
Having a quick bark at the lawn.

Billy begins to feel vomit creeping up his mouth and runs out the door.

SCENE 4 - SOLDIERS AT NIGHT

Private Brown and Neville are getting ready for bed.

NEVILLE
What do we do when we get them?

PRIVATE BROWN
Huh?

NEVILLE
The emus. I mean once we've...Eliminated them, what do we do? Just leave them on the ground? That doesn't sound very dignified does it? Do we bury them? Should we have a memorial at the end of the day or something to - to honour them?

PRIVATE BROWN
Major Meredith said we can use the emu skins and feathers for hats for the light-horse.

NEVILLE
Hats?

PRIVATE BROWN
Gotta get the most out of the amount of resources they're sending over.

NEVILLE
I don't think I'd feel very comfortable wearing an emu hat.

PRIVATE BROWN
How's it any different to wearing a hat made of cow?

NEVILLE
We wear hats made of cows?

PRIVATE BROWN
Leather.

NEVILLE
That's cow? Oh gosh. Oh my. So all those hats in the Great War were all made of cow?

PRIVATE BROWN
Yep.

NEVILLE
That's a lot of dead cows.

PRIVATE BROWN
A lot of dead men too.

Beat.

NEVILLE
Can I tell you something, Douglas?

PRIVATE BROWN
I'm a little tired -

NEVILLE
I don't think I'm destined to be soldier. I'm only doing it to make my parents happy.

PRIVATE BROWN
Neville -

NEVILLE
No, it's true, Douglas. I hate dirt and bugs and snakes, anything to do with the outdoors really. It terrifies me. And I hate conflict. If I'm totally honest with you, Douglas, I think I'd like to be a dancer.

PRIVATE BROWN
Uh-huh.

NEVILLE

But do my own moves, nothing like things you see in ballrooms. I'd like to express my feelings through the medium of dance. It's where I feel most comfortable. No words. Just expression through my limbs.

PRIVATE BROWN

Well maybe you should take a course or something when we get back. Now, Neville -

NEVILLE

No this is what I'm saying Douglas! The dance that's within me is not something that can be taught. It's of the moment. Put it in a category at your own peril. I'm fucking magic. Excuse my language.

PRIVATE BROWN

Could I - could I see something?

NEVILLE

What here? Now?

PRIVATE BROWN

Sure. Why not?

NEVILLE

No, no, no these aren't the right conditions, Douglas. No!

PRIVATE BROWN

Okay, okay. I was just asking.

NEVILLE
Yeah and you're part of the problem! You don't understand what's burning inside - I'm sorry, Douglas. I don't mean to take it out on you.

PRIVATE BROWN
It's okay, Neville. You're okay.

NEVILLE
Enough of this, we're here to kill the emus. We kill those emus and we get the respect we deserve.

PRIVATE BROWN
Alright then, goodnight Nev -

NEVILLE
Have you got a lady back home?

PRIVATE BROWN
No I don't I'm afraid.

NEVILLE
Neither do I.

PRIVATE BROWN
Embarrassingly I actually get quite nervous in the company of a beautiful woman.

NEVILLE
So do I! Well most people really.

PRIVATE BROWN
It's like I'm watching myself from the corner of the room trying to make conversation and I hate myself. Like, I'm good, I'm just working through some things, you know, to get to the source.

NEVILLE
Totally, totally. Introspection. Totally.

Billy appears at the edge of the room with vomit down his shirt.

BILLY
I could smash ya both.

Billy leaves.

PRIVATE BROWN
Goodnight, Neville.

NEVILLE
Goodnight, Douglas.

SCENE 5 - LEADERS

Sydney. The office of Major G.P.W. Meredith. He is flanked by serial suck up 'yes man' and humourless COLONEL WARWICK KATTER (40's).

Major Meredith is feeling his pants against his

leg and bottom.

MAJOR MEREDITH
Tell me, Colonel Katter -

COLONEL KATTER
Yes, sir.

MAJOR MEREDITH
Do you think I've put on weight?

COLONEL KATTER
Why no, sir. Not at all. You look rather lissom to me.

MAJOR MEREDITH
These pants, they're snug against my rump.

COLONEL KATTER
Who says that's a bad thing, Major? You have quite a nice rump indeed.

MAJOR MEREDITH
Yes. You're right. Notepad.

Colonel Katter whips out a notepad to take down Major Meredith's thoughts.

MAJOR MEREDITH
Item one to bring before Sir George Pearce upon our next meeting. Hem the pants around the upper thigh to give greater curvature to the bottom. A soldier should always dress to

impress. What do you think of that, Colonel Katter?

COLONEL KATTER
Wonderful idea, sir.

MAJOR MEREDITH
I don't know where they come from. It's amazing. Often I'll be sitting there, thoughtless, then knock-knock, thought arrives and huzzah! Genius.

COLONEL KATTER
That's why you're a Major, Major.

MAJOR MEREDITH
Indeed Colonel. I didn't get to the top by playing tiddlywinks. Although I'll never turn down a game of tiddlywinks.

COLONEL KATTER
Would you like to play, Major?

MAJOR MEREDITH
Not now, Colonel, we have business to attend to!

COLONEL KATTER
Of course. I just...If you ever want to play a game of tiddlywinks or any other game, I'm your man.

MAJOR MEREDITH
Good God man are you still talking about games? What is the matter with you?

COLONEL KATTER
Moving on, sir.

MAJOR MEREDITH
Give me an update on the emu project.

COLONEL KATTER
Word across the wireless is that our two men have arrived at Warralakin and are commencing the emu cull as we speak.

MAJOR MEREDITH
Very good. Capable soldiers?

COLONEL KATTER
Yes, sir, I believe so, sir. Private Douglas Brown, exemplary record has been put in charge of the cull and with him is Private Neville Kelly, son of Major Kelly, sir.

MAJOR MEREDITH
Major Kelly's boy. If he's anything like his father then the boy will probably talk the emus to death.

COLONEL KATTER
That seems unlikely, sir.

MAJOR MEREDITH
It's a joke, Colonel Katter.

COLONEL KATTER
Oh.

Colonel Katter forces out a laugh - it's very, very awkward and unnatural.

MAJOR MEREDITH
When are they expected back?

COLONEL KATTER
End of the week.

MAJOR MEREDITH
Fantastic, Colonel. We can put to bed those horrific looking wonky walkers once and for all.

COLONEL KATTER
Death to the emu, sir.

MAJOR MEREDITH
Indeed. Indeed, Colonel. Item number two. Should the pants flare at the lower leg?

SCENE 6 - DAY FINISHED

The back deck at Warralakin.

Day one has not gone as expected. Clementine lights a cigarette.

CLEMENTINE
Anyone want a dart?

PRIVATE BROWN
Please.

CLEMENTINE
Fast aren't they?

PRIVATE BROWN
Today was a good learning curve.

CLEMENTINE
How many did you get?

PRIVATE BROWN
All that matters is we've started.

CLEMENTINE
You didn't get any.

NEVILLE
We got four.

CLEMENTINE
Four? Four fucken emus.

NEVILLE
It's better than none.

CLEMENTINE
Marginally.

NEVILLE
I killed three of them.

PRIVATE BROWN
Shut up, Neville.

NEVILLE
All in a day's work. I didn't expect to get any. I've exceeded my expectations already.

CLEMENTINE
Killing four emus isn't going to stop the wheat getting nicked.

NEVILLE
No, but it's more of a personal achievement kind of thing.

PRIVATE BROWN
It's a start, madam. And you're more than welcome to come join us if you're worried about our future efficiency.

CLEMENTINE
Customs prevent me from fighting, Private. You know that.

NEVILLE
It's alright, with me on the team we'll get there.

PRIVATE BROWN
Don't get too cocky, Neville. It's day one, I'll catch you.

NEVILLE
I dunno, Douglas. You looked pretty hopeless out there. It's

okay, we can't be good at everything. You're handsome, remember?

                PRIVATE BROWN

And a good soldier.

                Small beat.

                PRIVATE BROWN

Hello! I am!

                CLEMENTINE

Do you like lamb?

                NEVILLE

Funny you ask that. No. It always leaves a funny taste in my mouth.

                CLEMENTINE

You haven't had my lamb.

                NEVILLE

Well I always like having my mind changed.

                CLEMENTINE

I'll knock Hillary off and roast her. We should really get a dog. It gets tiresome killing your pets.

                Billy enters with four beers.

BILLY

Jesus wept that was a pathetic display of marksmanship today. Who taught you lot how to hold a Lewis Gun, blind Freddy?

NEVILLE

I got three.

BILLY

You've gone through a thousand rounds of ammunition ya wally. I don't know much about maths but I reckon even my brother'd tell you the odds aren't good on that and he's as bright as a two watt bulb.

PRIVATE BROWN

We're just getting used to the way they operate.

BILLY

They're fucken flightless birds what do you mean the way they operate? They run. Shoot the pricks.

PRIVATE BROWN

It's not as easy as that.

BILLY

You've got a machine that shoots a bucket load of bullets, what's the problem?

PRIVATE BROWN

Only up to a certain range. We have to get within distance for the bullets to reach them.

NEVILLE
It's actually pretty hard.

BILLY
How do you feel Dougal? This bloke's running rings around you.

CLEMENTINE
The soldier on light duties.

NEVILLE
[*Chuckles*] I know! I can't believe it either!

BILLY
We're not complimenting you.

NEVILLE
I don't care it's just nice to feel good at soldier stuff.

CLEMENTINE
I'll tell you something for nothing, you're not leaving here any time soon. The rate you're going you'll be here till the mining boom.

BILLY
The what?

CLEMENTINE
Dunno just got a feeling something's coming.

NEVILLE
Hang on. Is there like - a number - a target we have to -when are

we...Done?

PRIVATE BROWN
There's no specific number.

NEVILLE
Then who do we know when we can go home?

BILLY
When the pricks stop eating our wheat.

NEVILLE
Huh. We might need some help, Douglas.

PRIVATE BROWN
You think, Neville?

NEVILLE
Hang on, have I offended you?

CLEMENTINE
I think the time to bring in reinforcements was yesterday.

PRIVATE BROWN
I'll get in touch with Sydney.

NEVILLE
I didn't want to offend you. Father said that men like to bully each other, it's a good way of making friends. But it doesn't come naturally to me.

BILLY
Tell them to bring more beer when they get here.

PRIVATE BROWN
I'm not sure I can -

BILLY
More. Beeyah.

NEVILLE
Oh no! I've hurt your feelings!

PRIVATE BROWN
Neville, shut up, you haven't hurt my feelings. I have a letter to write.

Private Brown leaves.

NEVILLE
We're besties so it's fun to tease each other. I know that.

Slight pause.

NEVILLE
I'm going to go for a little dance.

Neville exits.

CLEMENTINE
We're never leaving here are we? Come on Hillary, time to face the music.

SCENE 7 - FEEDBACK IN SYDNEY

Sydney. Colonel Katter is reading out letters addressed to Major Meredith.

COLONEL KATTER
'Dear Major Meredith,
I write to you concerning a matter of national safety -

MAJOR MEREDITH
Who's this from?

COLONEL KATTER
Major General Palmer.

MAJOR MEREDITH
Erght that bloated arse-licker. Bin.

COLONEL KATTER
He's a Major General, sir.

MAJOR MEREDITH
Major General, Major General - is that above or below me?

COLONEL KATTER
It's below, sir.

MAJOR MEREDITH
Bin.

COLONEL KATTER
It's just it sounds rather serious -

MAJOR MEREDITH
Bin. Next.

Colonel Katter gets out another letter.

COLONEL KATTER
'To Major Meredith,

MAJOR MEREDITH
Ugh I've got to stop eating so many carbs I feel bloated. Go on.

COLONEL KATTER
'I write to you in the hope you might be able to help me with a problem I have -

MAJOR MEREDITH
Bored. Bin.

COLONEL KATTER
We have a letter from Private Douglas Brown, sir.

MAJOR MEREDITH
Who?

COLONEL KATTER
He's in charge of the emu cull.

MAJOR MEREDITH
Oh good! Very exciting. Open it, open. Open, open, open!

COLONEL KATTER
'Dear Major Meredith,
I write to you from the ground here at Warralakin to inform you of our progress on the emu cull.'

MAJOR MEREDITH
This is exciting!

COLONEL KATTER
'Unfortunately, sir, our first day did not go to plan as expected and presented us with some rather worrying insights.'

MAJOR MEREDITH
Well that's not good.

COLONEL KATTER
'It seems, although flightless, the emu is quite a talented mover and shaker. The emu is presenting itself to be a rather masterful escape artist. The animal is very quick across the land and has managed to outmaneuver our weaponry on several hundred occasions. I ask that you consider sending more members of the Artillery in order to combat these deceptive birds.
Yours in earnest,
Private Douglas Brown.'

MAJOR MEREDITH
Bastards.

COLONEL KATTER
What do you want to do, sir?

MAJOR MEREDITH
I want to kill every emu in Australia.

COLONEL KATTER
Sir?

MAJOR MEREDITH
Well not every emu but, like, a lot of them. This is my mission, Katter. I have to prevail. We'll send every man we can. Who have we got?

COLONEL KATTER
Well...Resources are stretched relatively thin for this mission, sir.

MAJOR MEREDITH
Why?

COLONEL KATTER
The Great War, sir. A lot of men died.

MAJOR MEREDITH
Oh. Yes. Of course.

COLONEL KATTER
Sir, we did receive a letter of support from a Private Reginald Turner regarding our involvement in the conflict, if you recall?

MAJOR MEREDITH

Of course I do. 'Your service to the nation will not go unnoticed. If there's an opportunity to serve I would relish it.' Good lad. Send him. We need someone with that enthusiasm.

COLONEL KATTER

On it, sir.

SCENE 8 - NEW RECRUIT

The back deck. The sun is starting to go down on another disastrous day.

CLEMENTINE

Do you ever feel like the sun is getting hotter?

PRIVATE BROWN

I don't know. Isn't it always hot here?

CLEMENTINE

Every year it feels like I'm starting to sweat more and more.

NEVILLE

Maybe you're going through menopause.

CLEMENTINE

I'm not going through menopause you goose. I'm talking about the weather.

NEVILLE
I know but I read someone that when women go through menopause -

CLEMENTINE
Sorry are you explaining what menopause is to me?

NEVILLE
No. I - what were you saying before?

CLEMENTINE
When we first moved out here I don't remember it being this hot. I could cope with it. Now, I'm in a lather by the time I get to the letterbox.

NEVILLE
Who delivers your mail out here? Is it a weekly thing or...?

CLEMENTINE
Can't be normal this heat. It's bloody killing me. Hasn't rained in six months. Not a drop. Not a single drop.

NEVILLE
Rain's annoying anyway. You can't do anything when it's raining.

CLEMENTINE
We're growing wheat.

NEVILLE
I guess a bit of rain'd be good then.

PRIVATE BROWN
Could be around the corner.

CLEMENTINE
How did we get to this point in our lives, Neville?

NEVILLE
Oh, I'm not sure I'm equipped to answer that question.

CLEMENTINE
Sometimes I can't help but think to myself I wouldn't mind a random fuck. You know what I mean?

NEVILLE
Ah -

CLEMENTINE
Just a pointless, random, forgetful fuck. Just cast aside the fact I've got an alcoholic weight dragging me down and let loose.

NEVILLE
Clementine I should say if this is a proposition -

CLEMENTINE
Not with you Neville! Yuck.

NEVILLE
Yuck's harsh.

PRIVATE BROWN
I might get a beer.

Private Brown leaves.

CLEMENTINE
Just a casual rogering.

Billy enters.

BILLY
Just punched one.

CLEMENTINE
What?

BILLY
Emu. Punched it.

CLEMENTINE
Why?

BILLY
Eating the wheat. Punched it. When's the newbie getting here?

CLEMENTINE
Any minute.

NEVILLE
You punched an emu?

BILLY
Punched it in the head.

Private Brown enters with a beer.

CLEMENTINE
I don't understand why you punched it.

PRIVATE BROWN
What'd you punch?

BILLY
Emu.

PRIVATE BROWN
You punched it?

BILLY
It was eating the wheat, popped its head up, punched it.

PRIVATE BROWN
Why would you do that?

BILLY
What?

PRIVATE BROWN
What kind of a psychopath punches an emu?

BILLY
You're killing 'em by order of the government.

PRIVATE BROWN
Yeah as a duty. To stop them eating crops. I'm not going up to them like some pissed English tourist at the Coogee Bay looking for a biff.

BILLY
Why are you having a go at me for? I'm doing your job.

NEVILLE
Seems a little insensitive.

BILLY
Insensitive? They're fucken emus!

NEVILLE
I'm sure they feel.

BILLY
Yeah I gave them something to feel. My fist into their nogan.

CLEMENTINE
Tough stuff, Bill. Everyone's so impressed.

BILLY
I'm saving our crops.

PRIVATE BROWN
There's a way of doing things with dignity and then there's other ways and I think you chose the other way.

NEVILLE
Was it okay?

BILLY
Who cares? We're trying to kill them!

NEVILLE
Kind of makes you wonder why.

BILLY
The crops.

NEVILLE
I know but, they're not that bad are they?

BILLY
Yes!

CLEMENTINE
They're pretty bad.

NEVILLE
They were here first.

BILLY
Who's side are you on here people?

ALL
The emus.

On walks REGINALD/REGINA TURNER (20's).

PRIVATE BROWN
Private!

Neville checks his pants.

REGINA
Private Reginald Turner, reporting for duty.

CLEMENTINE
Hope you've brought your aim with you.

REGINA
Yes, ma'am, with the help of the Lewis gun I think we should have no problems defeating the enemy.

PRIVATE BROWN
This is Neville and I'm Douglas.

BILLY
Neville's a weird prick.

CLEMENTINE
Neville isn't weird. He's just not great socially, Bill. Christ have some manners.

BILLY
You don't reckon he's weird? Dougal?

PRIVATE BROWN
Private Kelly could be viewed as peculiar.

BILLY
Peculiar, that means weird doesn't it?

PRIVATE BROWN
Yes.

BILLY
See! Weird.

NEVILLE
Nice to meet you.

REGINA
They reckon they're fast. Hard to shoot.

PRIVATE BROWN
That's been one of the challenges, yes.

NEVILLE
If you'd like tips on how to best take down the enemy I'm your man.

PRIVATE BROWN
I think as long as we work as a team then we'll be able to achieve our goal.

BILLY
Normally I'd challenge newcomers to a wrestle but I just

punched an emu so I'm pretty worn out.

                REGINA

Why'd you punch it?

                BILLY

I'm not going through this again! Shit.

Billy storms off.

                CLEMENTINE

Do you think it's inappropriate of me to wish for another war? Did you bring beer?

                REGINA

Were we supposed to?

                CLEMENTINE

Great. If I have to be sober at any point I'm blaming you.

                PRIVATE BROWN

Are we out of beer?

                CLEMENTINE

We will be soon if I know I have to keep living here. I'm going for a lie down.

Clementine leaves.

                NEVILLE

She's great. I think we're bonding.

PRIVATE BROWN
How was the journey in?

REGINA
Fine, fine. Nothing out here.

NEVILLE
Right?

REGINA
Paper's reckon this is the biggest combat since The Great War.

NEVILLE
We're in the papers? I should start a scrapbook.

PRIVATE BROWN
There's a lot of work to do.

REGINA
Not much success so far I'm taking it?

NEVILLE
It can be colour coded.

PRIVATE BROWN
Not yet. We'll get there.

REGINA
Slippery bastards.

NEVILLE
And dated with little hand drawn pictures.

REGINA
Destroying the crops of our mighty veterans.

PRIVATE BROWN
The extra hands will go a long way.

NEVILLE
Even make copies, send one to father.

PRIVATE BROWN
Neville, do you mind?

NEVILLE
Not at all. At this point in time it's just a hypothetical scrapbook but you can have a copy too.

PRIVATE BROWN
We're in conversation here.

NEVILLE
Oh. Can I help?

PRIVATE BROWN
By being quiet for a moment, yes.

NEVILLE
He's just jealous cause I'm killing more emus than him.

PRIVATE BROWN
I'm not jealous.

NEVILLE
Oh okay pretty boy if you're so not jealous of me how about you take your shirt off?

PRIVATE BROWN
What?

NEVILLE
I've gotta go.

Neville exits.

PRIVATE BROWN
He means well. You're from Perth I hear?

REGINA
Is that a problem?

PRIVATE BROWN
No, I like Perth. It's nice.

REGINA
No one likes Perth. What's your game?

PRIVATE BROWN
No game.

REGINA
Last man we knew that had a bad word to say about Perth didn't turn out so well...Syphilis. Went mad. Coincidence?

PRIVATE BROWN
I'd say so.

REGINA
You'd like that wouldn't you?

PRIVATE BROWN
I don't know what you mean by that.

REGINA
Are we gonna have a problem?

PRIVATE BROWN
What? No.

REGINA
Cause if you want a problem I can give you a problem.

PRIVATE BROWN
No problems!

REGINA
You don't have any problems?

PRIVATE BROWN
Like, I've got some existential stuff rolling around at the moment, you know, my place in the world and all -

REGINA
Not those sort of problems, problems with me problems.

PRIVATE BROWN
Yeah, no, none of that.

REGINA
Yes or no?

PRIVATE BROWN
Should we just forget about it?

REGINA
Distraction, hey? Nice try. I think we should get to the bottom of this. Right now. I don't want any distractions.

PRIVATE BROWN
I can't see any distractions.

REGINA
Other than this.

PRIVATE BROWN
Then let's clear it up.

REGINA
You're not the boss here.

PRIVATE BROWN
Well, technically I'm in charge of the mission -

                    REGINA
No. We're equals. If we're a team then we're equals.

                    PRIVATE BROWN
Um. Okay.

                    REGINA
Great. Well, I'm going to get some shut eye.

          Regina leaves.

                    PRIVATE BROWN
Okay.

          SCENE 9 - NIGHT TERRORS

          Night time. The Privates are all asleep when suddenly Neville sits bolt upright and screams:

                    PRIVATE BROWN
Neville! What are you doing?

                    NEVILLE
What are you looking at you beast?

                    PRIVATE BROWN
Neville!

                    NEVILLE
I'm only doing as I'm told.

REGINA
What's going on?

PRIVATE BROWN
I don't know.

NEVILLE
I'm just following orders.

PRIVATE BROWN
Neville, wake up!

REGINA
He's sleeping?

PRIVATE BROWN
I don't know!

NEVILLE
It's not my fault! I'm sorry!

PRIVATE BROWN
Neville!

Private Brown shakes Neville awake.

NEVILLE
Douglas!

PRIVATE BROWN
Neville!

NEVILLE
Why are you cuddling me? I appreciate it but -

PRIVATE BROWN
I'm waking you, Neville. You were having night terrors.

NEVILLE
I was?

PRIVATE BROWN
Are you alright?

NEVILLE
Well, yes, I think so. What happened?

PRIVATE BROWN
I think you were seeing...Emus.

NEVILLE
Huh. Curious, hey, Douglas?

PRIVATE BROWN
So, you're okay?

NEVILLE
Yes, yes! I'm good - I'm just happy to be here, happy to do what's asked of me. Got some new friends here to help.

NEVILLE
I really should get some sleep, Douglas. I'm quite tired. Killed three emus today. Goodnight.

SCENE 10 - WAR RAGING ON

Billy & Clementine on the back deck.

BILLY
They're elusive, Clem. The way they move...So goofy, so bloody effective. The new one looks like a dead eye dick but still, the birds, they're fast. I seen Reginald hit a target from a hundred yards but it was stationary. These birds are all –

Billy jumps up and down, limbs going everywhere.

BILLY
How do you shoot that, Clementine?

CLEMENTINE
Quite easily.

BILLY
We need more help. They're going through all the ammo and we've got hardly an emu head to show for it.

Regina comes on.

REGINA
They're pretty elusive.

Private Brown comes on.

PRIVATE BROWN
The bastards are so elusive.

Neville comes on.

NEVILLE
Another pretty good day from me.

PRIVATE BROWN
I can't - I can't - I'm doing my best but they're...I need liquor.

CLEMENTINE
Billy.

BILLY
You know where the beers are.

PRIVATE BROWN
I need something harder.

BILLY
Shame. Only got the beers.

CLEMENTINE
Get them some whisky.

BILLY
I don't have -

CLEMENTINE
Do I have to find it myself?

BILLY
It's mine, Clem.

CLEMENTINE
I'm going to count to three.

BILLY
That's not gonna do anything.

CLEMENTINE
One.

BILLY
I don't care about your counting.

CLEMENTINE
Two.

BILLY
Don't care.

CLEMENTINE
Th -

Billy runs off stage to get the whisky.

PRIVATE BROWN
I don't know what to do with myself.

REGINA
You'll figure it out.

PRIVATE BROWN
How are you so relaxed about this?

REGINA
Dunno. Just not in Perth so that's a plus.

PRIVATE BROWN
I thought you loved Perth?

REGINA
Perth's alright, it's just - never mind.

NEVILLE
Are you on the run?

REGINA
No.

NEVILLE
He's a crim.

REGINA
No I'm not.

NEVILLE
A crim!

REGINA
I'm not a criminal, Neville. I just had...Personal - shut up, Neville.

Billy returns with whisky.

BILLY
So I found this lying around somewhere but that's all I've got so…

Private Brown snatches the bottle off Billy and finishes it off.

BILLY
Me fucken giggle juice! CLEMENTINE YOU DIDN'T LEAVE ANY FOR ME!

PRIVATE BROWN
Sorry.

CLEMENTINE
Do you know how many beers I have to drink to get pissed, Brown?

BILLY
I was saving that for a rainy day.

CLEMENTINE
Hasn't rained in six months Billy you idiot!

BILLY
Exactly! What are we gonna celebrate with now ya turd.

REGINA
You can do better than him, you know?

BILLY
Better than me? Pigs fart you can.

REGINA
You're not trapped. Like, you can leave.

CLEMENTINE
It's not that simple.

PRIVATE BROWN
What if we fail?

BILLY
Go on then. Leave.

CLEMENTINE
Where would I go? What would I do?

REGINA
There's plenty of work in Perth.

CLEMENTINE
Really? Perth?

REGINA
It gets a bad wrap but I reckon you'd be able to find a job and a house pretty easily. Rent's low and I can't see it going up much. There's a wealth of cultural festivities in the city centre.

CLEMENTINE
In Perth?

BILLY
See if I give a shit.

REGINA
Yes! In Perth!

PRIVATE BROWN
Nothing feels in our control.

NEVILLE
I kill emus.

CLEMENTINE
It's just I never really saw leaving a husband as a viable option.

REGINA
I know people who have done it. It's doable.

CLEMENTINE
Huh. Worth thinking about.

BILLY
Woah, woah, woah -

REGINA
Shoot on through.

NEVILLE
Shoot, Neville. That's what they're saying. Shoot! Shoot to kill! It's for the good of the country, Neville. You're a killer. A killer.

PRIVATE BROWN
Neville?

NEVILLE
A murderer. A killer - killer - killer -

PRIVATE BROWN
Neville.

NEVILLE
It's in your blood, Kelly! You're a natural born killer.

REGINA
Oh here we go -

NEVILLE
THE BLOOD!

BILLY
KEEP IT TOGETHER, MAN!

NEVILLE
Hats, we're making hats -

PRIVATE BROWN
Get me some water.

Clementine gets Private Brown some water.

NEVILLE
Little feathers out of the cadaver.

Private Brown throws water on Neville's face.

NEVILLE
S'pose that's as good as speaking to a psychologist.

PRIVATE BROWN
Neville, are you back?

NEVILLE
Better than ever!

PRIVATE BROWN
This war...I need to write to Sydney.

CLEMENTINE
We need more liquor.

                    REGINA
And the Lewis Guns aren't enough.

                 PRIVATE BROWN
No. No, we need to step this up.

                    NEVILLE
Step, ball, kick. Step, ball, kick! I'm a prancer, fella.

                 PRIVATE BROWN
Maybe some more men too.

                     BILLY
Tough ones.

SCENE 11 - TOUGH MEN

Major Meredith is sipping on a glass of champagne in his Sydney office, winged by Colonel Katter.

                 MAJOR MEREDITH
Fruity, sweet and inoffensive with a pleasant odour. An all round people pleaser.

                 COLONEL KATTER
Sir -

                 MAJOR MEREDITH
Oh what now, Colonel?

COLONEL KATTER
It's just, I think there's a better way to start.

MAJOR MEREDITH
All right then, what?

COLONEL KATTER
Major Meredith is a man of principals.

MAJOR MEREDITH
...That is a good start.

COLONEL KATTER
Stoic when necessary, kind when hardship presents itself.

MAJOR MEREDITH
It's just so...bland. I mean they all start the same way. Captain blah blah was very good in war blah blah. This needs my essence.

COLONEL KATTER
I understand.

MAJOR MEREDITH
Do you? Cause sometimes it feels like you just tell me what I want to hear.

COLONEL KATTER
That's only because I respect you so much, sir.

MAJOR MEREDITH
You respect me?

COLONEL KATTER
More than anyone in the world.

MAJOR MEREDITH
Do you like me?

COLONEL KATTER
Uh-huh.

MAJOR MEREDITH
How much?

COLONEL KATTER
Lots.

MAJOR MEREDITH
More than your parents?

COLONEL KATTER
Oh.

MAJOR MEREDITH
Well, like, I'm kind of more important to you than them, right?

COLONEL KATTER
Um.

MAJOR MEREDITH
Like, I'm a bit of a mentor...

COLONEL KATTER
Yes, I, I like you more than my parents.

MAJOR MEREDITH
And you think I'm a good Major?

COLONEL KATTER
The best.

MAJOR MEREDITH
Better than Major Morrison?

COLONEL KATTER
A million times better.

MAJOR MEREDITH
Good. Well it's obvious isn't it? I mean he's just so ergh and I'm so wow, you know?

COLONEL KATTER
Oh yes.

MAJOR MEREDITH
So we have to find a middle ground. Sensible enough that it looks professional but still jazzy so it has a bit of character. It really has to pop if it's in the playbill.

                    COLONEL KATTER
I agree.

                    MAJOR MEREDITH
Good. Should we take five?

                    COLONEL KATTER
If you like.

                    MAJOR MEREDITH
It might help productivity. Clear the head a little.

                    COLONEL KATTER
Yes, sir.

                    MAJOR MEREDITH
I like this champagne it makes me all giddy.

                    COLONEL KATTER
Sir, while we're taking a moment I feel as though I should update you on some of our actual work.

                    MAJOR MEREDITH
Actual work?

                    COLONEL KATTER
That's not what I meant.

                    MAJOR MEREDITH
Art isn't actual work to you, Colonel Katter?

COLONEL KATTER
No, of course -

MAJOR MEREDITH
What is it?

COLONEL KATTER
The emu's sir.

MAJOR MEREDITH
Aren't they dead yet?

COLONEL KATTER
Not quite.

MAJOR MEREDITH
Well what's the hold up?

COLONEL KATTER
It appears as though the birds are craftier than we could have ever imagined sir. From all reports it's having quite an impact on the men.

MAJOR MEREDITH
Impact in what way?

COLONEL KATTER
Apparently Private Kelly is...Going quite mad, sir.

MAJOR MEREDITH
Oh grow a pair, Kelly.

COLONEL KATTER
I'm not sure that's so helpful -

MAJOR MEREDITH
I'VE HAD BRAIN SPLATTERED ON MY FACE, COLONEL! THESE ARE BIRDS!

Beat.

MAJOR MEREDITH
I'm sorry. How many have we killed.

COLONEL KATTER
The returns are...modest.

MAJOR MEREDITH
How modest?

COLONEL KATTER
Could count on fingers and toes, modest.

MAJOR MEREDITH
Dear.

COLONEL KATTER
Dear, indeed, sir.

MAJOR MEREDITH
Pesky, pesky, birds.

COLONEL KATTER

Private Brown suggested that the Lewis Guns weren't sufficient, sir.

MAJOR MEREDITH

I see...

COLONEL KATTER

What should our next course of action be, sir?

MAJOR MEREDITH

Well...A problem ignored is a problem enhanced wouldn't you say, Colonel?

COLONEL KATTER

Yes I would, sir.

MAJOR MEREDITH

When I put it to parliament that this war is essential I never imagined that we could possibly...I mean we won the Great War for goodness sake's and now we can't even...Christ! The nation needs this victory, Colonel. We need to up our attack.

COLONEL KATTER

More ammunition, sir?

MAJOR MEREDITH

Not just that, Colonel. I think it's time to send in the Infantry Tank Mark II.

COLONEL KATTER
The Matilda, sir?

MAJOR MEREDITH
She'll sort out the enemy. As will I. For in times of grave uncertainty people need a leader. They need a face they can follow. Pack your best summer gear, Colonel. We're headed to Warralakin.

SCENE 12 - SLEEPING

Late at night. Private Brown is having a cigarette.

REGINA
Can't sleep, huh?

PRIVATE BROWN
No I...My mind is elsewhere.

REGINA
It's a lot to process. It's tough out here. They're not an easy kill.

PRIVATE BROWN
Yeah, yeah. Yeah, for sure. Yep. Yep. Yep. Totally. Yep.

Beat.

PRIVATE BROWN
I mean I guess the bigger is, though, like...Who am I? Right? Like, am I just a soldier? Am I just a man? Am I, you know, in

the grand of scheme of things, I'm nothing, right? We're all nothing. History, there's no way I'm going to be remembered. You're not going to be remembered. None of this will be remembered. And that's probably a good thing, right? This will just come and go and everyone will forget this War. But then also, people will forget us. If I have kids - I don't even know if I want to have kids. Who am I to have kids? It's a tricky world. Maybe I shouldn't bring kids into it. But say if I did and they had kids and they had kids then I'm just...Some guy that lived a few generations before to them. Right? So, I guess, like, the world, the universe, universes - cause there are more - we're not the only ones. What does it matter? Anything, what does anything matter?

          REGINA

Right.

          Slight pause.

          REGINA

So, I was only coming out to pee but, this sounds kind of...Big. For you.

          PRIVATE BROWN

It's pretty cool what you've done.

          REGINA

Sorry?

          PRIVATE BROWN

Like, you wanted something and you went and got it.

REGINA
What are you talking about?

PRIVATE BROWN
Women aren't allowed to fight and you are. So kudos to you.

REGINA
I'm not a woman.

PRIVATE BROWN
Yes you are.

REGINA
You are.

PRIVATE BROWN
No, I'm not.

REGINA
I'm not though.

PRIVATE BROWN
Okay.

Beat.

REGINA
You tell anyone and I'll cut your throat.

PRIVATE BROWN
Why would I tell anyone? It's your business.

Neville enters.

NEVILLE
Time to go again?

PRIVATE BROWN
It's the middle of the night, Neville.

NEVILLE
Good-o.

Neville exits.

REGINA
If anyone finds out they'll send me back to Perth and I can't go back there.

PRIVATE BROWN
Oh so Perth's not so good then?

REGINA
My ex-husband's there.

PRIVATE BROWN
Ohhhhhhh -

REGINA
Yeah.

PRIVATE BROWN
Ohhhhhhh I see. Right.

REGINA
So, like, tricky.

PRIVATE BROWN
Totally. I mean, it's your life. You gotta what's right for you.

REGINA
I have.

PRIVATE BROWN
And that's awesome.

Clementine enters.

CLEMENTINE
What's awesome?

PRIVATE BROWN
Onion marmalade!

CLEMENTINE
There's absolutely no way you were talking about onion marmalade.

PRIVATE BROWN
What are you doing up?

CLEMENTINE
Billy's snoring. What's awesome?

REGINA
She's not going to tell anyone, it's fine.

CLEMENTINE
That you're a woman?

REGINA
Yep.

CLEMENTINE
Why would I tell anyone? It's your business.

REGINA
Exactly.

PRIVATE BROWN
That's a good thing, honesty. That's a value. I should list my values.

CLEMENTINE
Christ you're not losing it too are you?

PRIVATE BROWN
No, no, no, no, no - nup. Nup. No. Well, it's tricky cause -

REGINA
Go for a walk.

PRIVATE BROWN

Good idea. Sift through - it's a lovely night. And there are stars in the sky. Lots of stars. More than my little brain can comprehend. My small, small, insignificant - see you in the morning.

Private Brown exits.

CLEMENTINE

If you weren't here we'd hardly have an emu to show for all the bullets. At least one of you is more than competent.

REGINA

Raw talent, I suppose.

CLEMENTINE

Lucky to have you. Plus you look great in that uniform.

Beat.

There's a moment between the two of them.

CLEMENTINE	REGINA
Better get some shut eye.	I've gotta pee.

SCENE 13 - REINFORCEMENTS

The arrival of Major Meredith and Colonel Katter.

Major Meredith and Colonel Katter are both dressed in very short shorts while Colonel Katter is struggling with the luggage.

MAJOR MEREDITH
This heat is ugly.

COLONEL KATTER
There's a certain amount of inner thigh rubbing one can stand in a day and I'm afraid I've reached my quota. My thighs are red raw, sir.

MAJOR MEREDITH
The shorts look great don't you think?

COLONEL KATTER
On your shapely legs, certainly.

MAJOR MEREDITH
I should've brought some for the fellas but it didn't even cross my mind. I've been so busy.

COLONEL KATTER
Yes.

MAJOR MEREDITH
They go well with the shoes.

COLONEL KATTER
They do.

MAJOR MEREDITH
Little secret.

COLONEL KATTER
Please.

MAJOR MEREDITH
Prada. I know.

COLONEL KATTER
Oh, Major.

MAJOR MEREDITH
It's a bit naughty. You know because the Italians are our enemy and everything.

COLONEL KATTER
But so worth it.

MAJOR MEREDITH
Right?

COLONEL KATTER
They're glorious.

MAJOR MEREDITH
I know. I just had to.

COLONEL KATTER
Of course you did!

MAJOR MEREDITH
I'm such a glutton for Italian leather.

COLONEL KATTER
You want quality.

MAJOR MEREDITH
Careful don't scuff them.

COLONEL KATTER
Sorry.

MAJOR MEREDITH
On second thought this should probably be my nighttime shoe. Can you get me the little booty numbers?

COLONEL KATTER
Certainly.

Colonel Katter opens up the suitcase and looks for the boots.

MAJOR MEREDITH
The Australian landscape is truly a sight to behold isn't it? I often find myself marvelling at all the different colours.

Colonel Katter finds the boots.

COLONEL KATTER
Here we are, sir.

Major Meredith lifts on leg for Colonel Katter to remove his shoe.

MAJOR MEREDITH
You know when the first white settlers arrived in Australia from England the artists were unable to capture the colours of the landscape in their paintings. They painted the trees as if they were willows back in England.

Major Meredith lifts his other leg.

MAJOR MEREDITH
Of course for the fifty thousand years prior to that there were already artists here doing it justice but for some reason we still fail to properly acknowledge the cultural importance - Ow! Careful, Colonel.

COLONEL KATTER
Apologies, sir. This one's a little tight.

MAJOR MEREDITH
I'm not fat.

COLONEL KATTER
I'm not saying -

MAJOR MEREDITH
I'm trying to cut the carbs I told you!

COLONEL KATTER
There. They're much better.

MAJOR MEREDITH
Yeah I feel more rugged in these. Like I could do a little pounce on something.

COLONEL KATTER
Yes they're more butch.

MAJOR MEREDITH
Oh don't say butch, Colonel. We're about to be in a war. Cut out the camp would you, darling - Colonel.

COLONEL KATTER
Yes, sir.

MAJOR MEREDITH
Remember they need to be lead and they best respond to a firm hand a masculine figure.

Clementine arrives.

MAJOR MEREDITH
Oh my God look at you.

CLEMENTINE
What?

MAJOR MEREDITH
You're a vision. Look at you. Are the lady of the house?

CLEMENTINE
You could call me that.

Billy enters.

MAJOR MEREDITH
Enchante. Look at that dress.

BILLY
Are you French?

MAJOR MEREDITH
Mmph?

CLEMENTINE
This is Billy.

COLONEL KATTER
I like the name Billy.

BILLY
Righto.

MAJOR MEREDITH
Where are the soldiers?

BILLY
Round the back.

Major Meredith hollers out:

MAJOR MEREDITH
COOWEE! MEN! They'll come here now just after that. Look.

Private Brown, Regina and Neville enter.

MAJOR MEREDITH
Oh what a funny little gang we've got here. Hi all. I'm Major Meredith and this is Colonel Katter.

COLONEL KATTER
Hiya, gents.

MAJOR MEREDITH
Look I think I'm going to keep it simple. We all know why we're here. We've just got to put our best foot forward and, you know, be better than nature. That being said I'm also a fun guy and I like to have a good time as much as the next person don't I, Colonel?

COLONEL KATTER
He does.

MAJOR MEREDITH
So let's enjoy ourselves.

BILLY
Did you bring any booze?

MAJOR MEREDITH
Party boy over here.

CLEMENTINE
No, seriously, did you bring any booze?

MAJOR MEREDITH
Only a suitcase full. Thank me later. Or thank me now.

He nods to the gang as if to prompt them to thank him.

ALL
Thank you.

MAJOR MEREDITH
You're welcome.

COLONEL KATTER
He's a very good leader.

MAJOR MEREDITH
Stop it.

BILLY
Get off it you suck up.

CLEMENTINE
You must be buggered.

COLONEL KATTER
Oh yes.

MAJOR MEREDITH
I'm surprisingly invigorated.

BILLY
Give us the piss.

COLONEL KATTER
Maybe we should drop the bags off -

NEVILLE
My name's Neville!

Beat.

PRIVATE BROWN
This is Private Kelly, Privates Turner and I'm Private Brown.

MAJOR MEREDITH
Neville's a bit of a spark plug isn't he?

NEVILLE
They'll turn 'em into hats.

MAJOR MEREDITH
Right. I don't know that means. Shall we?

BILLY
Give. Me. The. Piss.

MAJOR MEREDITH
Okay, here we go. Tonight, we drink. Tomorrow we slaughter! Hoorah!

SCENE 14 - EMU'S DISCUSS

Out of the darkness appear figures, long legs, long necks...Puppet like figures moving through the space. We see them bend down and pick at the ground.
They come into focus - these are RON (played by the same actor as Private Brown), and DON (played by the same actor as Neville) - two emus. They move as emus would - limby and awkward. They graze.

DON
Seriously, what are they playing at?

RON
Dunno, mate.

DON
They're fucking hopeless.

RON
I know. Useless.

DON
Don't they realise we know these parts better than they ever will?

RON
Up themselves, Don.

DON
Bloody oath. I mean, for fuck's sake, aren't we on the coat of arms?

RON
The what?

DON
On the money and that.

RON
We are?

DON
Yeah, mate. National bloody treasure. We're icons.

RON
Guess that'd make you the most famous Don in Australia.

DON
Invincible, mate.

They continue to graze.

DON
Sorry to harp on about this -

RON
You're right.

DON
But, I mean, those loud machines they've got - what's that all about? Just one of the little nuggets and we're gone.

RON
You hear they got Damo?

DON
Damo? Oh, not Damo. He was hilarious. Ugly bastard but a good laugh.

RON
They've got no class, mate. None at all.

Out of nowhere we see a kangaroo KERRY-ANNE (played by the same actor as Clementine).

KERRY-ANNE
Ooroo.

RON
How ya traveling, Kerry-Anne?

KERRY-ANNE

I'm fine. What's going on with you guys? Those pricks are teeing off on you. What's that about?

RON

Couldn't tell you. They just starting going off one day.

KERRY-ANNE

I don't understand. What have you done? You were minding your own business, weren't you?

RON

It's a mystery to us, Kerry-Anne.

DON

You lost anyone?

KERRY-ANNE

They're not going after roos.

DON

What? Why?

KERRY-ANNE

Dunno. That's what I wanted to ask you.

DON

Oh this is bullshit.

KERRY-ANNE

Well I hope you know that we've got your back. I mean, we're on the bloody coat of arms together for fuck's sake.

     RON
The coins and that. How are the kids?

     KERRY-ANNE
Don't get me started. Olly's being a turd. Some days I wonder why I had them. Make sure you don't rush it.

     DON
I can't have kids. Ripped my gonads off on a wire fence. Looked like two watermelons hanging from a piece of dental floss.

     KERRY-ANNE
Well on that note I'm gonna head off. I gotta check if Steve and Mark are still throwing down.

     RON
The twins still at each other?

     KERRY-ANNE
It's unrelenting.

     RON
Well make sure you're looking after yourself.

     KERRY-ANNE
I've got my mental health check list. You take care too. Ooroo.

     RON
Ooroo.

DON
Ooroo.

Kerry-Anne leaves.

RON
Better get a wriggle on, Don.

DON
After you, Ron.

They run into the darkness. Blackout.

INTERVAL

ACT 2: MAN VS NATURE

SCENE 1 - MATILDA ROLLS IN

Out of the darkness we hear the sound of choral singing - all the soldiers at once:

'Once a jolly swagman camped by a billabong,
Under the shade of a Coolibah tree,
And he sang as he watched and waited till his billy boiled,
You'll come a Waltzing Matilda with me.'

Out of the darkness appears the Infantry Tank Mark II aka the Matilda - a 1930's tank. Major Meredith stands atop the tank striking a Napoleon type image as the other soldiers flank the tank.

'Waltzing Matilda, Waltzing Matilda, You'll come a-Waltzing Matilda with me.
And he sang as he watched and waited till his billy boiled,
You'll come a Waltzing Matilda with me.'

The tank comes to a halt centre stage. Private Brown and Turner jump off with their Lewis guns and begin to set them up.

'Down came a jumbuck to drink at that billabong,
Up jumped the swagman and grabbed him with glee,
And he sang as he shoved that jumbuck in his

tucker bag, You'll come a Waltzing Matilda with me.'

Colonel Katter jumps off and looks through binoculars. Neville goes to the back of the tank and begins to load ammunition as Private Brown and Turner load their weapons.

'Waltzing Matilda, Waltzing Matilda, You'll come a-Waltzing Matilda with me.
He sang as he shoved that jumback in his tucker bag, You'll come a-Waltzing Matilda with me.'

All the weapons are loaded. They all look to Colonel Katter who raises his arm:

'Up rode the squatter, mounted on his thoroughbred,
Up rode the trotters, one, two, three
With that jolly jumbuck you've got in your tucker bag? You'll come a-Waltzing Matilda with me.'

Colonel Katter drops his binoculars and looks to Major Meredith. Not yet.

'Waltzing Matilda, Waltzing Matilda, You'll come a-Waltzing Matilda with me.
With that jolly jumbuck you've got in your tucker bag? You'll come a-Waltzing Matilda with me.'

Meredith looks out. Colonel Katter looks through his binoculars once more. He raises his arm:

'Up jumped the swagman and sprang into the billabong, You'll never take me alive, said he –'

Colonel Katter indicates to shoot. The singing stops and gunfire rings out towards the audience.

It is prolonged. It goes and goes – the sound crescendos and we hear the faint sound of white noise:

Blackout.

SCENE 2 - END OF DAY

Late at night.

Major Meredith is at the centre of attention as he demonstrates some of his dance moves, some real boot scootin' stuff.

By this stage they've been drinking for some time, some holding their liquor better than others. Neville is off to the side by himself, clearly very drunk.

MAJOR MEREDITH
It's all about the hips.

CLEMENTINE
You're quite the mover.

MAJOR MEREDITH
I was a ballroom dancer as a child.

BILLY
Fuck me.

COLONEL KATTER
Do you still remember how to ballroom dance?

MAJOR MEREDITH
Oh no one wants to see that.

REGINA
Oh yes we do.

MAJOR MEREDITH
Oh I don't know.

REGINA
Go on! Wouldn't we all like to see it?

ALL	BILLY
Yes!	No.

MAJOR MEREDITH
Well I'll need a partner.

COLONEL KATTER
I'll do it.

MAJOR MEREDITH
Traditionally it's with a lady.

COLONEL KATTER
Who cares about traditions?

MAJOR MEREDITH
Colonel -

COLONEL KATTER
What? We're all open minded people here aren't we?

BILLY
How open?

CLEMENTINE
I'm happy to sit this out.

REGINA
Same here.

PRIVATE BROWN
[*Covering Reginald's mistake*] SAME!

MAJOR MEREDITH
Well, okay. Shall we?

COLONEL KATTER
Yes. We. Shall.

Colonel Katter stands ready to be led by Major Meredith.

Major Meredith approaches. It's all quite delicate, slow. Then...They begin to ballroom dance. It's a little awkward. It's not as fluid as it should be. Colonel Katter is playing catch up.

NEVILLE
Lame! Shit! Lame! It's all structured! No feeling!

Private Brown dashes to Neville's side. Colonel Katter and Major Meredith stop dancing.

PRIVATE BROWN
Neville, buddy, they're just having a little dance.

NEVILLE
That's not a dance. They don't know the meaning of it.

MAJOR MEREDITH
Excuse me, Private?

NEVILLE
You think just cause you know a couple of steps you know what it means to dance? You're a phony, pal.

COLONEL KATTER
How very dare you speak to Major Meredith like that.

NEVILLE
You too kiss arse.

PRIVATE BROWN
You'll have to forgive Private Kerry-Anne. He's perhaps over indulged a touch.

COLONEL KATTER
Shall we resume, Major?

MAJOR MEREDITH
Yes, yes, we should, Colonel.

They resume dancing.

BILLY
Christ, I feel ill.

Regina and Clementine, aside.

REGINA
I've gotta give it to Meredith, he can move.

CLEMENTINE
Those hips...

REGINA
Shapely.

CLEMENTINE
Supple.

It's clear they're no longer talking about Major Meredith.

REGINA
Sumptuous.

CLEMENTINE
A gorgeous...

NEVILLE
Is there even any feeling there?

CLEMENTINE   REGINA
No!   No!

COLONEL KATTER
Oh, definitely.

NEVILLE
Can't see it! Not impressed! Have you got a club foot or something?

COLONEL KATTER
Excuse me?

NEVILLE
You're dragging your left foot.

COLONEL KATTER
I am not!

MAJOR MEREDITH
You are, Colonel. I must admit this isn't as I was hoping.

COLONEL KATTER
But, sir -

MAJOR MEREDITH
You're dismissed, Colonel.

COLONEL KATTER
Buggity bugger!

Colonel Katter leaves in a huff.

NEVILLE
You wanna see a real dance?

PRIVATE BROWN
Ahhh Neville -

NEVILLE
With emotion! Feeling! Pain!

Neville leaps out in front of everyone.

NEVILLE
Someone count me in.

CLEMENTINE
Three, two, one.

Neville begins to move. It's...Interpretive. Full of emotion. Earnest as all fuck.

PRIVATE BROWN
Nice work, Neville.

NEVILLE
Not done.

Neville continues to move. Now with more gusto.

BILLY
What am I watching?

MAJOR MEREDITH
I underestimated you, soldier. That was a thing of beauty.

NEVILLE
If there's one thing I do well it's express myself through movement.

Private Brown pats Neville on the shoulder.

PRIVATE BROWN
Well done -

NEVILLE
ARGH! AMBUSH!

Neville runs off stage.

MAJOR MEREDITH
The dance is powerful in that one. I think I should make a toast. Thus far the mission has been a difficult one, I'm aware. However, I earnestly believe we have reason for optimism moving forward.

We have some terrific marksmen and many thousand more rounds of ammunition. I say we get these emu's terminated in time for Christmas and enjoy a well earned break. What do you say? To the mission.

ALL
To the mission.

They all drink.

MAJOR MEREDITH
Private Brown, what did you think of my dancing? Your opinion matters the most of course because you're the best looking person here.

PRIVATE BROWN
Is that the effect I have on people? Make them run away?

MAJOR MEREDITH
Private, my dancing.

PRIVATE BROWN
Exquisite, sir.

MAJOR MEREDITH
You're just saying that.

PRIVATE BROWN
Yes, I am. I didn't like it.

MAJOR MEREDITH
Poo poo to you then.

COLONEL KATTER
You complete asshole.

MAJOR MEREDITH
It's okay, Colonel.

PRIVATE BROWN
I didn't want to - maybe I am an asshole. Am I an asshole? I've never really thought about it before. People have always been kind to me but have I been kind to them in return? Is everything I've been led to believe about myself a lie? Am I an asshole? Don't answer that. That's a question I need to ask of myself. Only I can find the truth...An asshole...

Private Brown leaves.

CLEMENTINE
This is all normal stuff.

COLONEL KATTER
I'd just like to clarify, sir, your dancing is exquisite.

BILLY
What the fuck are we still talking about you prancing about, chief? Can we talk about something else?

MAJOR MEREDITH
Certainly. What would you like to talk about?

BILLY
Footy and that.

MAJOR MEREDITH
Oh the football! Do you play?

BILLY
No.

MAJOR MEREDITH
Did you when you were younger?

BILLY
Yep. Weapon.

CLEMENTINE
Billy -

BILLY
No, Clem.

MAJOR MEREDITH
What position?

BILLY
Um. I played -

CLEMENTINE
Billy was never picked in the side. He ran the waters.

BILLY
I did not!

CLEMENTINE
You were in the papers for being the water boy that got concussed when you ran into the goal post.

BILLY
I was trying to get out of the way of Johnny the Axe!

CLEMENTINE
Instead you just axed yourself.

BILLY
I'm a fucking legend why are you all so mean to me? This is bullshit. I'm gonna punch a tree.

Billy leaves.

MAJOR MEREDITH
Darl, you deserve better.

CLEMENTINE
Blind Freddy could see that.

MAJOR MEREDITH
I knew a blind Freddy once. He died of leprosy the poor dear. Great set of legs...For a while.

COLONEL KATTER
Probably not as good as yours, sir.

MAJOR MEREDITH
Well no one's legs are as good as mine, Colonel.

COLONEL KATTER
Do you like my legs, sir?

MAJOR MEREDITH
Colonel, professional, please.

COLONEL KATTER
Yes, sir. Sometimes I get a little lost in your - lost in the - in the...Heat. Goodnight.

Colonel Katter leaves.

MAJOR MEREDITH
To be a leader of men, hey. Deary me.

Major Meredith leaves. It's just Clementine and Regina now. A few moments pass - there's a serious sexual tension in the air.

CLEMENTINE
From all reports you're the best soldier here.

REGINA
You've heard that have you?

CLEMENTINE
Yes, I have.

REGINA
I'd like to think I'm capable of impressing.

CLEMENTINE
Mission accomplished.

They both laugh awkwardly.

CLEMENTINE
Hot isn't it?

REGINA
Boiling.

CLEMENTINE
All this clothing in this heat. Wowza.

REGINA
I can't tell you how good it feels to take my clothes off at the end of the day.

Beat.

CLEMENTINE
I'm going to have a cup of tea.

REGINA
I'm going to go for a power walk.

CLEMENTINE
See ya.

REGINA
Yep.

They both hurry off.

SCENE 3 - THE PANEL

Don and Ron are joined by PRISCILLA (played by the same actor as Regina).

RON
Thank you for joining us, Priscilla.

PRISCILLA
Pleasure. It's good to check in about all this.

DON
They're bloody assholes! I can't fucking stand it anymore. I'M GOING TO GO INSANE!

RON
Alright, Don. We know. It's tough out there for all of us.

PRISCILLA
I just want to know what we've done.

RON
I think we're beyond that now, Priscilla. We just need to figure out how to solve this.

DON
I know how we solve it. We go in there and peck the fuck out of the cruel bastards. See how they like that.

RON
Your anger is warranted, Ron. But we need to get practical and you know that's not a viable option.

PRISCILLA
It doesn't seem like they're going to let up any time soon. They've brought in a bigger noise machine.

RON
On the plus side the ratio seems to be in our favour.

DON
One emu dead is one too many.

RON
I'm just trying to find some positives, Don. They do seem to struggle with a manic scatter. Maybe if we continue down that line we'll break their will. Realistically they've only got the mid-section to aim at.

PRISCILLA
I'm a little worried about that to be honest. I've put on a couple.

RON
Really?

PRISCILLA
Yeah, I'm overeating. I thought cause I'm exercising as much as I do I'd be fine. But you know they say, it's eighty percent diet.

RON
You'd never know, Priscilla. You wear it well. Sorry I shouldn't comment on your appearance.

PRISCILLA
No, no that's fine. Thank you I appreciate it. Look, it's nearly the end of the year. I'll probably just keep going the way I am, what with Christmas coming up.

RON
Oh, yeah, I mean, we all overeat over Christmas. And that's okay.

PRISCILLA
New Year's resolution.

RON
I can never stick to mine.

PRISCILLA
Neither.

DON
Sorry, what the fuck are we talking about New Year's

resolutions for? We're getting murdered.

Kerry-Anne hops in.

KERRY-ANNE
Having another meeting are we?

RON
Trying to come up with a plan of attack.

DON
Defence more like it.

RON
Have you two met?

KERRY-ANNE
We haven't. I feel like I've seen you around but I can't place where.

PRISCILLA
Yeah, you look familiar. Do you hang out near the shrubbery about twenty k's north west?

KERRY-ANNE
No, that's my twin sister. I hang out in the east mostly.

PRISCILLA
I don't spend much time in the East. Feels a bit stuffy.

KERRY-ANNE

No, I get that. But it's nice once you adjust.

PRISCILLA

OH! I know where I've seen you. The three eucalyptus trees!

KERRY-ANNE

Yes!

PRISCILLA

I knew I'd seen you somewhere.

RON

Good date spot the three eucalyptus trees. That being said the last date I had there was a complete fizzer.

PRISCILLA

Really?

RON

Yeah we just didn't click. I felt like I was driving the conversation the whole time.

PRISCILLA

I hate that.

KERRY-ANNE

Tell me about it. I went on a date with a bloke called Gary about a month ago. Hardly said a work. Great root though.

PRISCILLA
Sometimes you just need a good rogering, right?

KERRY-ANNE
Oh totally. I wasn't going on a second. And I think he knew that. I bumped into him once after and it was kind of awkward but I mean, what can you do?

PRISCILLA
Just gotta do what's best for you.

DON
Can we get back on track, please?

KERRY-ANNE
I'll leave you to it.

Kerry-Anne hops away.

RON
What were we talking about?

PRISCILLA
Weight. Have you heard of keto?

DON
No! No, this is bullshit. We're chit chatting about fucking weight loss and we're out there getting killed. Killed! Why aren't you taking this more seriously? I mean, what's it going to take? Yesterday I watched Mary bleed to death as her children watched on. They've lost a mother and you're concerned about putting on

a few kegs? This is serious. Those kids are orphans now. And we can dance around it as much as we want but we are in danger and aren't doing anything about it. How many dying is it going to take before you pull your heads out of your arse and really evaluate this situation?

Cause I sure as shit don't wanna see any more orphaned children because these people are hell bent on taking us down.

Beat.

DON
None of us want to die do we?

RON
No, mate.

DON
I'm sick of running scared. I'm sick of seeing my friends die. The pain...And I don't know about you but I'm terrified. And if you're not then you're lying to yourselves.

Pause.

PRISCILLA
I'm scared too, Don.

DON
I don't wanna live like this anymore. We've done nothing to deserve this. I've gotta go clear my head.

Don leaves.

PRISCILLA
I hate to admit it...But this might not be okay. We could be in trouble here.

RON
I know.

SCENE 6 - TEA TIME

Regina and Clementine are sitting on the back deck having a cup of tea. Both of them sip at the same time. Sexual tension is rife.

REGINA
That's a good cuppa.

CLEMENTINE
Nothing like a good cuppa.

REGINA
I'll tell you the worst tea? Earl grey. Tastes like soap.

CLEMENTINE
It does!

REGINA
Can't trust an earl grey drinker.

CLEMENTINE
I really feel like the tea game is going to explode one day.

REGINA
In what sense?

CLEMENTINE
Your English breakfasts, your chamomile's, your peppermints - they'll be boring. It'll be all sorts of different blends.

REGINA
I'd welcome spicing things up a bit.

CLEMENTINE
As would I.

Beat.

They sip their tea.

CLEMENTINE
Yep that's a good cuppa.

Billy enters.

BILLY
Think you're right, Clem. Think we're up shit creek without a paddle. Numbnuts here's the only one doing anything right.

REGINA
Yeah, look, it's pretty challenging. It's not from lack of effort though.

CLEMENTINE
No, I'm sure it isn't.

REGINA
It's just hard to focus sometimes. In the heat.

CLEMENTINE
I find it helps me focus.

REGINA
Focus on what?

CLEMENTINE
Whatever I feel like focusing on.

REGINA
You like to focus?

CLEMENTINE
I love it.

BILLY
The fuck are you two talking about?

CLEMENTINE
Focusing! The mission! The War!

BILLY
Not a matter of focus you just gotta shoot the pricks. When I was in France -

CLEMENTINE
Billy...

BILLY
When I was in France we knew how to kill. Oh, we knew how to kill alright.

CLEMENTINE
Very good.

BILLY
Oh, we knew how to kill alright.

CLEMENTINE
We heard you.

BILLY
Oh, we knew how to kill alright.

CLEMENTINE
Yes, Billy, we know.

BILLY
Oh, we knew how to kill alright.

Beat.

BILLY
Dunno what happened there. Must've blacked out. Better grab a beer.

Billy exits as Private Brown enters.

PRIVATE BROWN

At some point you're just left questioning the point of it all. The futility. Do you know what I mean? We're hardly killing any of them. Our returns per bullet are disastrous and it just makes you think. It makes you think about our role in all this. In the world. As humans. Co-existing with nature. What's that about? What are we about? What's life about?

Private Brown exits.

REGINA

They're good these men, aren't they?

CLEMENTINE

I've seen worse. I once had a dalliance with a returned soldier who's weapon had been smashed to smithereens by shrapnel. It was like having sex with a handful of oysters poorly wrapped in cling film.

REGINA

That is...Immensely graphic.

CLEMENTINE

You want graphic? Imagine staring that thing in the eye. I don't know why we're talking about previously observed penises.

REGINA

We're not. You are.

CLEMENTINE
Let's cut it off then. The conversation not - you know.

REGINA
Yep.

Pause.

REGINA
I don't know how much longer I can keep doing this.

CLEMENTINE
What?

REGINA
You know what.

CLEMENTINE
Fighting? It must be draining.

REGINA
It is.

CLEMENTINE
Then stop.

REGINA
I don't know if it's that simple.

CLEMENTINE
It is.

They kiss.

Billy returns just in time to miss them kissing.

BILLY
Should we get a dog?

SCENE 7 - NEVILLE REBOUNDS

Major Meredith is journaling. Private Brown enters.

PRIVATE BROWN
Oh, Major, sorry I'll come back -

MAJOR MEREDITH
No, you're fine, Private. I was just scribbling down some thoughts. Come.

PRIVATE BROWN
Thinking of plans?

MAJOR MEREDITH
Stream of consciousness prose.

PRIVATE BROWN
Uh-huh.

MAJOR MEREDITH
Would you like to hear some?

PRIVATE BROWN
That's okay.

MAJOR MEREDITH
'I stand tall, taught, terrific. The harsh Australian landscape stares back at me. She's beautiful. Her face dabbed with a delightful rouge. The motley bunch around me look for guidance. They're as serious about this mission as I. No silly buggers or wet willies. They're as hard as a rock protruding from a heaving bush.' Thoughts?

PRIVATE BROWN
Lovely. Very...Evocative.

MAJOR MEREDITH
That's what I thought. I'm very artistic, you see. Would you like a lolly? I'm quite naughty sometimes.

Major Meredith reveals a small handful of lollies.

PRIVATE BROWN
I'm fine.

MAJOR MEREDITH
Have a lolly.

PRIVATE BROWN
I'm okay.

MAJOR MEREDITH
Have a little lolly.

PRIVATE BROWN
I don't want one.

MAJOR MEREDITH
Just one little lolly.

PRIVATE BROWN
Really, I'm good.

MAJOR MEREDITH
Oh indulge me, Private!

PRIVATE BROWN
Fine.

Private Brown takes a lolly from Major Meredith. He pops it in his mouth.

MAJOR MEREDITH
Aren't they tantalizing?

PRIVATE BROWN
They're quite good, yes.

MAJOR MEREDITH
I'm a bit of a wordsmith don't you think? Yes, I've always loved language. I'm probably best served being a poet rather than a Major.

Major Meredith begins to cry.

PRIVATE BROWN
Hey, hey...It's okay.

Major Meredith fans his eyes.

MAJOR MEREDITH
No it's not. They're on top of us, Private. These stupid birds are killing me. I don't want to use hyperbole but I'm literally dying.

PRIVATE BROWN
Sir, please. You're not dying. You're steering the ship. Admittedly it's a very hard ship to steer and I'm not sure if we'll ever - that's not the point. You're doing everything you can.

MAJOR MEREDITH
You don't understand, Private! I know what everyone thinks of me. I'm responsible for the death of thousands of men in The Great War. Everyone thinks I'm a nincompoop. A little nincompoop with great legs. This is my chance to redeem myself.

PRIVATE BROWN
Well then you just have to remain positive.

MAJOR MEREDITH
It's not beyond that? We can still do it?

PRIVATE BROWN
Sure.

MAJOR MEREDITH
Oh look at me carrying on like a big girls blouse.

PRIVATE BROWN
We all have our moments, sir.

MAJOR MEREDITH
Yes that's true. And we are killing more.

PRIVATE BROWN
We are.

MAJOR MEREDITH
And you think I'm a good Major?

PRIVATE BROWN
Yes, sir.

MAJOR MEREDITH
How good?

PRIVATE BROWN
Good.

MAJOR MEREDITH
The best Major ever?

PRIVATE BROWN
Let's just settle down.

MAJOR MEREDITH
I sincerely appreciate your optimism, soldier. Sometimes I get a little in my head. A bit anxious. And then once that snowball starts goodness it's hard to catch. Realistically we are doing much better. And I believe that I'm getting an understanding as to how the emu thinks.

PRIVATE BROWN
How the emu thinks...

MAJOR MEREDITH
Mmm...See thing, get thing. Very straight forward. Logical brains. Which is actually very useful for me. I've started using a calendar. Adhering to more structure. You know us creative brains...I'm sorry for showing my vulnerable side. Though I do think it's important for us fellas to cry sometimes. I have emotions. And they're valid.

PRIVATE BROWN
Where's Colonel Katter, sir? I never see you without him.

MAJOR MEREDITH
He and I had a little tiff. It'll be fine. We just need some space.

PRIVATE BROWN
Bad, sir?

MAJOR MEREDITH
He asked to borrow the Prada's and I told him he doesn't have the calves for them. He'll get over it.

Regina enters.

REGINA
I just thought I should let you know that Neville is currently in a heated argument with a tree.

MAJOR MEREDITH
So eccentric.

PRIVATE BROWN
Sir, do you think it might be an idea to check on him?

MAJOR MEREDITH
It's more fun out here.

PRIVATE BROWN
Yes, but, you are the leader.

MAJOR MEREDITH
Oh! Of course. Leader of men. I should set the example shouldn't I?

PRIVATE BROWN
Probably, sir.

MAJOR MEREDITH
Here comes your hero, Neville.

Major Meredith exits.

PRIVATE BROWN
Can I tell you something, Private? I don't think...I don't know who I am.

REGINA
What?

PRIVATE BROWN
This isn't me. There's got to be something...I don't know what I'm saying.

Clementine enters.

CLEMENTINE
Oh. Hey you two.

REGINA
Hey! How's it going?

CLEMENTINE
Oh, you know. Pretty good.

REGINA
That's good.

CLEMENTINE
Emu's are a bugger aren't they?

REGINA
Total bugger.

Major Meredith re-enters.

MAJOR MEREDITH
No, no, that man's batshit.

Neville comes charging on.

NEVILLE

I killed an emu, Daddy! I killed many an emu! Ten times more than Douglas! I'm a good soldier, Daddy!

PRIVATE BROWN

Neville?

NEVILLE

Hello, father.

PRIVATE BROWN

Neville, it's Douglas.

NEVILLE

Good one.

PRIVATE BROWN

You know us, Neville. This is Regina, remember?

NEVILLE

Oh you're the one that's in love with Clementine.

REGINA

I'm not in love with her!

NEVILLE

I see the way you look at her. I see everything.

                    REGINA
Shut the fuck up idiot.

                    CLEMENTINE
Do you?

                    REGINA
No! I barely like you.

                    CLEMENTINE
Woah.

                    NEVILLE
Ouchy wowah!

                    REGINA
No, that's not -

                    NEVILLE
Damage is done. Damage. Damage. Damage. Someone's digging a deep grave. Funny little fella, I am.

                    MAJOR MEREDITH
You two are in love? How charming.

                    CLEMENTINE
Apparently she doesn't even like me.

                    MAJOR MEREDITH
She?

REGINA
Oh fuck.

MAJOR MEREDITH
You're a woman?

NEVILLE
Are you deaf, dumb and blind you big gimp?

MAJOR MEREDITH
Look, you, that's not very nice.

NEVILLE
I'm sick of being the nice guy. No one gives a shit about me.

PRIVATE BROWN
That's not true, Neville.

MAJOR MEREDITH
So that would make you two...

Billy enters.

REGINA
Lesbians, yes.

BILLY
Love 'em.

CLEMENTINE
You idiot.

BILLY
This again.

MAJOR MEREDITH
How terrific is this? See, I'm a cosmopolitan man. Love is love you delicious little things.

NEVILLE
Sucks to be Billy, right?

BILLY
It's awesome being me. I'm a champion. I've got fists that can cut through concrete.

MAJOR MEREDITH
Such machismo is unattractive these days, Billy.

BILLY
Whatever you just said - I disagree.

MAJOR MEREDITH
How am I supposed to deal with this?

BILLY
How about you focus on what you're supposed to deal with, Major? What are they going to say when you get back to Sydney if you lose this war? Especially after the shitshow you ran in The Great War.

MAJOR MEREDITH
Excuse me?

BILLY
What? You don't think we talk? My mates died at the hands of your incompetence you cunt. And if you don't pull your fucking finger out you're going to starve us to death so why don't you fucken do something?

Beat.

PRIVATE BROWN
Major -

MAJOR MEREDITH
No. No, he's right. I have to do something.

Major Meredith exits.

BILLY
I, um, sometimes it gets the better of me.

NEVILLE
Tell me about it. Everything's got the better of me forever. What a thing to say. Gosh I say some funny things. I'm a hoot. A hootananny. A riot. Should we riot? What for? Who against?

PRIVATE BROWN
Neville, come back.

NEVILLE
Neville is confused.

PRIVATE BROWN
You're okay, Neville.

CLEMENTINE
So…Like, nothing?

REGINA
I panicked. We're building, right? I mean - you know, like -

NEVILLE
Sorry are we talking about love or the construction industry? ZING!

PRIVATE BROWN
Come back, Neville.

NEVILLE
Do emus cry? I cry.

PRIVATE BROWN
NEVILLE! HERE!

NEVILLE
Hello, Douglas.

PRIVATE BROWN
Look at me.

NEVILLE
Handsome boy.

PRIVATE BROWN
Can you feel your feet on the ground?

CLEMENTINE
It's a little, I dunno, upsetting I guess.

NEVILLE
Yes.

BILLY
Hang on, are you two on?

PRIVATE BROWN
What else can you feel?

NEVILLE
Tension.

PRIVATE BROWN
Where?

NEVILLE
Between this lot.

PRIVATE BROWN
Focus on your body.

CLEMENTINE
We'll talk later, Billy.

PRIVATE BROWN
What can you feel?

NEVILLE
A little sweat.

BILLY
You are!

REGINA
We're not.

CLEMENTINE
We're not?

REGINA
I'm just trying to diffuse the situation.

PRIVATE BROWN
Where's the sweat, Neville?

NEVILLE
The pocket of skin between my testicles and my rear end.

PRIVATE BROWN
Shit.

NEVILLE
No, just sweat.

BILLY
Am I going mad here?

NEVILLE
You're in good company, fella.

PRIVATE BROWN
Neville, centre yourself. Close your eyes. Take a deep breath. Are you here with me?

NEVILLE
Yes, father.

CLEMENTINE
Fuck this.

REGINA
Clem -

Clementine exits.

PRIVATE BROWN
Neville...It's your friend Douglas. Open your eyes.

NEVILLE
Hi, Douglas.

PRIVATE BROWN
You're here with me now aren't you?

NEVILLE
Yes.

PRIVATE BROWN
Neville...You're a good man.

NEVILLE
Thank you, Douglas.

PRIVATE BROWN
No, Neville. Really hear me. You're a good man.

NEVILLE
I heard you.

PRIVATE BROWN
No, Neville. You're a good man. And you're loved.

NEVILLE
Uh-huh.

PRIVATE BROWN
You're loved, Neville.

NEVILLE
What are you doing?

PRIVATE BROWN
You're loved. And it's not your fault.

NEVILLE
Okay.

PRIVATE BROWN
It's not your fault.

NEVILLE
I feel like I've seen this before.

PRIVATE BROWN
You're your own man. And you're loved.

NEVILLE
...Do you love me?

PRIVATE BROWN
Yes, Neville. There's more to life than being a good soldier. Love, Neville. Friendship. You're loved, Neville.

By now both Private Brown and Neville are holding back tears. They embrace with gusto:

NEVILLE
Thank you, Douglas.

PRIVATE BROWN
Thank you, Neville.

             NEVILLE
Was that awesome to watch?

             BILLY
Ragers.

SCENE 7 - REVENGE

Major Meredith sits atop the Matilda in the middle of the night. We hear the sound of crickets.

His hands are shaking.

He looks across the expansive land. He drops his head onto the gunner – exasperated.

He steadies himself and looks out again. He grips the gunner tightly. Tighter.

He bangs his fists down on the machine in a fit of rage.

His chest begins to heave – the weight of failure hitting him.

He steadies himself once more – now with an intense resolve.

He grips the machine – incredibly still

He begins to shoot an endless amount of bullets – the sound reverberates around the expansive land. He is filled with emotion and begins to cry as the sound of bullets cascade out.

The sound of crushing metal stops the gunfire. There's clunk after clunk. The gunfire has stopped.

The lights begin to fade.

It begins to rain - at first sprinkling then becoming heavier and heavier as the lights fade to black.

SCENE 8 - REPERCUSSIONS

Lights come up on Ron and Priscilla standing over the bloodied and crumpled corpse of Don.

Ron bends down and pokes at Don – he doesn't move.

   PRISCILLA
Brave.

   RON
Yeah. The poor prick. Look at him.

   PRISCILLA
He did what no other would.

RON
He shouldn't have had to go like that.

PRISCILLA
No...

Pause.

PRISCILLA
I guess if there's any positive to come out of this it looks like he destroyed the machine.

RON
He did?

PRISCILLA
I heard it. It sounded like screaming, then it all stopped and smoke billowed out.

RON
You brave bastard.

Kerry-Anne enters.

KERRY-ANNE
So it's true, hey?

RON
Unfortunately so, Kerry-Anne.

KERRY-ANNE
...Not much you can really say is there?

RON
Not really. But I suppose we should.

Ron steadies himself.

RON
Don did what not of us had the guts to do. He took on our enemy head first. He wasn't willing to sit idly by and continue to let us be slaughtered. I don't think I'll ever know how you mustered the strength to do what you did. Don...I just don't know how I'm ever going to get this image out of my head...

At times he wasn't an easy bird. We all knew of his temper, his brashness, but that's what made Don, Don. Beneath those feathers was a heart of gold. He loved all of us. He cared. Probably too much. And that's what made him my friend.

I will miss you immensely, Don. We will never forget the sacrifice you made in order to protect the others in your community. You are a hero. Rest easy, my friend.

Ron pulls away.

RON
This is fucked. Look at him. Look at what they've done to him! Those bastards! How is this fair? What have we done? Nothing! Look at him!

Beat.

RON
This is never going to end.

PRISCILLA
I thought that maybe Don doing what he did...Maybe destroying – I dunno, maybe it'd finish it.

KERRY-ANNE
You've gotta maintain that resilience.

RON
You think this'll end it? Look what happened last time things weren't going their way. Did they give up? No, they sent in bigger weapons, more power, more men. This isn't going to end a thing. This'll only make them angrier.

PRISCILLA
No, no, they've been bettered again. They're done.

RON
This war started out of nothing – you really think two setbacks is enough to end this torture? Use your fucking head, Priscilla.

PRISCILLA
Yeah cause you know everything don't you, Ron, you pious fuck.

KERRY-ANNE
Guys.

RON

Pious? Sorry someone here is trying to lead!

PRISCILLA

And look what good you've done. You cost Don his life. Blood is on your soul.

KERRY-ANNE

That's enough!

RON

How fucking dare you...

PRISCILLA

See it now, do you?

KERRY-ANNE

THAT'S ENOUGH!

Beat.

KERRY-ANNE

What are you doing? Look at yourselves. This is exactly what they want. If you start combusting from the inside, losing patience, losing cohesion then they'll win. And I don't think either of you are ready to give up just yet. Are you? Are you ready to lose your lives to these monsters? If you're not going to do it for you then do it for Don. I thought you were both better than this.

RON
The fight is over, Kerry-Anne...We're done.

KERRY-ANNE
No, no don't you –

RON
All we've got now is our last moments. And, yeah, that sucks. It really sucks. But I'm not gonna sit here and pretend anymore. Cause what's the point? Our attitude has to change. If we're going to enjoy any more time in our lives then we have to accept what's happening.

Pause.

PRISCILLA
I think you're right.

KERRY-ANNE
What are you talking about?

PRISCILLA
They're filled with hate. As much as it pains me...Shit.

KERRY-ANNE
Guys...

RON
We had it good for a long time.

PRISCILLA
Yeah. We did.

RON
All good things come to an end.

KERRY-ANNE
Maybe there's something we can do.

RON
No. It's okay, Kerry-Anne. It is what it is.

KERRY-ANNE
I...We'll miss you.

Kerry-Anne leaves.

PRISCILLA
I shouldn't have said –

RON
It's fine.

PRISCILLA
What should we do?

RON
Have a feed.

PRISCILLA
I'm still a bit bloated – what am I talking about? Let's pig out.

RON
Maybe a swim.

PRISCILLA
Yeah...A nice meal and the water...That sounds lovely.

RON
And we'll think of Don.

PRISCILLA
We'll think of all of them.

SCENE 9 - THE WAR IS OVER

All are on stage bar Major Meredith and Colonel Katter – there is a sense of resignation amongst the group.

Major Meredith enters with Colonel Katter trailing behind carrying an abundance of alcohol.

MAJOR MEREDITH
I have an announcement. I've sent word across the wire...After the kamikaze mission of one certain emu in which he destroyed our Matilda we have decided to end the war. We are done.

BILLY
Done?

MAJOR MEREDITH
We simply cannot defeat them. The war is forfeited.

BILLY
You're forfeiting the war against a bunch of emus?

MAJOR MEREDITH
That's right. Colonel Katter has alcohol. I suggest you drink.

PRIVATE BROWN
And they've accepted our resignation, sir?

MAJOR MEREDITH
There is no use having a correspondence, Private. My decision is final. They're too good.

COLONEL KATTER
Beer, sir?

MAJOR MEREDITH
Carbs, Katter. I'll have the vodka.

BILLY
You've got vodka!?

MAJOR MEREDITH
A smidge.

BILLY
Why didn't you tell me?!

MAJOR MEREDITH
Because you would've drunk it.

BILLY
Fucken oath I would've. Give us a nip.

MAJOR MEREDITH
You have beer.

NEVILLE
Forfeited...

MATTHEW
Good call. We're getting flogged.

BILLY
I. Am. Thirsty. I. Want. To. Get. Fuck. Eyed.

MAJOR MEREDITH
Give the man a beer, Colonel.

BILLY
I'M HARD GIVE ME SOMETHING HARD!

MAJOR MEREDITH
If you drunk enough beer you'll get sufficiently drunk, Billy.

Billy snatches a beer off Katter. He skulls it.

BILLY
Another.

CLEMENTINE
Haven't you already been drinking anyway, Billy?

BILLY
Yes. Of course I have. I'm not a pansy. I had my first beer at breakfast with my wheaty-bix.

PRIVATE BROWN
When do we leave, sir?

MAJOR MEREDITH
Tomorrow.

NEVILLE
We're getting out of here! Yippee!

CLEMENTINE
Tomorrow?

MAJOR MEREDITH
There's no reason to stick around, madame.

NEVILLE
You know what? I'm going to have a beer. A full beer. Cause I'm a big boy. Chuck us a brewski, Colonel.

COLONEL KATTER
Get one yourself, Neville.

NEVILLE
Keep your tights on.

MAJOR MEREDITH
I would like to thank everyone for their commitment to the mission.

COLONEL KATTER
You're welcome.

MAJOR MEREDITH
And I will be recommending a medal of honour for you all.

NEVILLE
A medal! Well that's better than all my participation awards.

MATTHEW
It's the army equivalent of a participation medal, Neville.

NEVILLE
Well add it to the pile! This is the best day of my life.

Reginald has a quiet word with Private Brown.

REGINALD
Are you okay?

PRIVATE BROWN
I'm great. We get to go home. Warralakin isn't all it's cracked up to be.

BILLY
Righto. I'm talking now!

CLEMENTINE
Always elucidating.

BILLY
Eluca-who?

CLEMENTINE
Dating.

BILLY
We're married.

CLEMENTINE
Elucidating.

BILLY
Who's Eluca? Is that your little pet nickname for what's-it's-face?

CLEMENTINE
The word is elucidating.

BILLY
What word?

PRIVATE BROWN
The word she's saying is elucidating, Billy. It means to make something clear.

BILLY
Are you two in cahoots?

PRIVATE BROWN
What?

BILLY
Elucidating all over me. I got you pegged, Brown.

PRIVATE BROWN
We're not in cahoots. I'm clarifying. A word that means clarifying.

CLEMENTINE
Seems pretty futile.

BILLY
Stop saying words I don't know! Can't we speak English?

CLEMENTINE
That is English.

BILLY
Not the English I know.

CLEMENTINE
How are we supposed to know what English you know?

BILLY
You know what English I know.

CLEMENTINE
Not really, Billy. I'm not inside your head.

BILLY
You know what I can understand. You know my favourite word.

CLEMENTINE
I do...

BILLY
Sausage. It's funny. Two s's'. Double meanings. That's a laugh. That's a good word. Why can't we just say sausage?

CLEMENTINE
Because we're not talking about sausages.

BILLY
We should be. They're bloody great.

MAJOR MEREDITH
I don't mind a sauso.

NEVILLE
Here's an interesting question. Do you put the sauce in the fridge or cupboard?

COLONEL KATTER
That's not an interesting question.

NEVILLE
Okay, here's another one. If you could have only three toes which would you choose?

MAJOR MEREDITH
I'd start with my big boy, then my pinky...Maybe the long the skinny one next to my big boy.

COLONEL KATTER
That's such a wonderful coupling, sir.

BILLY
I knew a bloke with no toes. Jimmy dancer did him in.

MAJOR MEREDITH
After they amputated his toes?

BILLY
They didn't amputate his toes. Got bitten by a shark.

CLEMENTINE
No he didn't.

BILLY
That's what he told me.

CLEMENTINE
Every second person in Western Australia reckons they've been bitten by a shark.

BILLY
Why the fuck are we talking about toes?

CLEMENTINE
It's more interesting than anything you'd have to offer.

BILLY
Christ! Aren't you supposed to support your husband?

CLEMENTINE
S'pose I am. That's a problem isn't it?

BILLY
Ken oath.

CLEMENTINE
Probably an indication it isn't working.

BILLY
Ken oath.

CLEMENTINE
Probably an indication my mind's gone elsewhere.

BILLY
Ken oath.

CLEMENTINE
Probably means I should leave.

BILLY
Ken - what?

MAJOR MEREDITH
Go you, lady!

CLEMENTINE
Yeah. I'm out.

BILLY
But but but –

NEVILLE
Get it out, fella.

BILLY
Piss off, spare dick.

NEVILLE
What'd you call me?

BILLY
Spare dick.

NEVILLE
Right. If I hear you say that one more time -

BILLY
Spare di –

Neville punches Billy in the face.

BILLY
You punched me in the face.

NEVILLE
Yes I did.

Billy launches himself towards Neville. Private Brown comes over and coat hangers Billy sending him skittling to the ground.

BILLY
STREWTH. ME BACK!

Billy writhes around on the ground in pain.

PRIVATE BROWN
I played in first grade, water boy.

NEVILLE
Douglas...You saved me. How can I ever repay you?

PRIVATE BROWN
Don't worry about it, Neville. It's what friends are for.

NEVILLE
Wow...I've never done a punch before. It felt quite good standing up for myself. Yes, good work, Neville.

COLONEL KATTER
That. Was. Hot.

Beat.

COLONEL KATTER
I mean it's quite hot isn't it?

Neville begins to feel his limbs move.

NEVILLE
It's happening...

He starts to feel the dance coming on.

NEVILLE
I HAVE TO DANCE!

Neville leaps off stage.

Major Meredith steals a moment with Colonel Katter.

MAJOR MEREDITH
Well that was quite exciting wasn't it?

COLONEL KATTER
Just a little bit, sir.

MAJOR MEREDITH
You know, Colonel, if it wasn't for you I don't know how I

would've got through this whole ordeal.

COLONEL KATTER
It's been an honour.

MAJOR MEREDITH
Maybe...You should come over for a roast pork some time.

COLONEL KATTER
Sir?

MAJOR MEREDITH
I do a mean crackling.

COLONEL KATTER
Your pork would be the most wonderful gift anyone could give me.

A moment.

MAJOR MEREDITH
I might slip into the booties.

COLONEL KATTER
I have to change my underwear.

Major Meredith and Colonel Katter exit.

BILLY
Can someone help me up?

REGINA
How do you feel?

CLEMENTINE
...Relieved.

REGINA
So you should be.

PRIVATE BROWN
We're actually leaving. It's actually happening. We're doing it.

REGINA
What are you gonna do?

PRIVATE BROWN
No idea. Something. I'm gonna watch Neville.

Private Brown leaves.

CLEMENTINE
Should we have a cup of tea?

REGINA
No Earl Grey.

CLEMENTINE
Anything but Earl Grey.

BILLY
I'll have a cuppa.

                    CLEMENTINE
After you.

                    REGINA
Thank you.

Regina and Clementine leave.

                    BILLY
Hey! Hey! Where are you going? Can someone help me? Hello?

Beat.

                    BILLY
Better used to this, Billy.

He is struck with melancholy before a flash of joy hits him.

                    BILLY
Ha! Sausage.

SCENE 10 - MEREDITH ADDRESSES PARLIAMENT FOR THE FINAL TIME

Major Meredith stands in front of the audience. He clears his throat.

                    MAJOR MEREDITH
Little tickle. Members of parliament I'm here before you today

to inform you that we conceded in our war against the emus. What originally looked like a fairly straight forward mission turned out to be anything but. Our opponent was crafty, stealthy and had wonderful legs that would spring them across the arid Earth rapidly. A man could only dream of those – I mean they had legs up to here. Obviously the rest of the animal isn't particularly aesthetically pleasing but I think it's important to acknowledge – anyway.

We did our best. We fought. And the soldiers that were out there did so gallantly. For their service to the war I recommend the soldiers receive a medal of honour.

              VOICE (OFF)
It's the emus that deserve a medal, dipshit.

              MAJOR MEREDITH
Classy, Roger. Can I just say my little coda without interruption please? Goodness me it's like pulling teeth standing up here in front of you nitwits sometimes. I leave you with this. As we move forward let us not forget this lesson...Ah, I'm tired. We're all tired. And fighting seems so futile when...I'm sorry.

I do have one recommendation. The hemming on the uniforms isn't flattering. These soldiers work their rumps off. If you've got it flaunt it. All those in favour say, yay!

SCENE 11 - THE EMUS WIN

The sound of the cackling laughter of kookaburras. It's then joined with the sound of laughter – Priscilla, Ron and STEVE (played by

Katter, a baby emu).

RON
What a bunch of useless nitwits!

PRISCILLA
Didn't I say Mother Nature would always win? Didn't I say that?

STEVE
They're so silly.

PRISCILLA
Oh it feels good doesn't it? Feel that fire running through your feathers? BOOM MUTHAFUCKERS! How about that guy in the short shorts? What a twat.

STEVE
I thought they looked quite fetching on him.

PRISCILLA
Shut up, Steve, he looked like a twat.

RON
Hey, united front. Leave the fighting to them.

PRISCILLA
Sorry, Steve.

STEVE
That's okay. When I grow up I'll just kick your arse.

PRISCILLA
No you won't.

STEVE
Wanna bet?

RON
You two. Enough. We won.

PRISCILLA
Do you think anyone'll ever find out about what happened?

RON
I think they'd be too ashamed to tell anyone wouldn't they?

PRISCILLA
Probably. Word gets out though, right? You hear Warren and Lucille have been having a thing?

STEVE
Lucille's having a thing with that busted old head?

PRISCILLA
His neck does things to her.

STEVE
His neck looks like a rotted scrott.

RON
Jesus Christ, Steve. Where'd you learn how to talk like that?

STEVE
Don.

RON
Well then you get a pass on that then.

PRISCILLA
Who would've thought it, hey? If it wasn't for Don...Who knows?

Kerry-Anne hops on.

KERRY-ANNE
What's up legends?! You did it! Seriously, what a bunch of idiots. Didn't they realise that Mother Nature will always win?

PRISCILLA
THAT'S WHAT I SAID!

KERRY-ANNE
Well on behalf of all of us, thank you. Who knows, they may have gone after us if they got all you. So, you know, given us a real pep in our step.

PRISCILLA
You're glowing, Kerry-Anne.

KERRY-ANNE
Yeah well the other thing...I'm up the duff.

PRISCILLA
No way! Congratulations!

KERRY-ANNE
Thank you, yeah, very exciting.

PRISCILLA
Who with?

KERRY-ANNE
Dunno I've been fucking for Australia.

RON
Have you started thinking about names?

KERRY-ANNE
Don't ask that to a pregnant roo, Ron. Gets a bit tedious.

RON
Sorry.

KERRY-ANNE
But if it's a boy we're going with Darren and if it's a girl we're going with Doreen.

PRISCILLA
Cracker names.

KERRY-ANNE
They run in the family. I just got lucky. And I tell you what I'm just grateful my kids are going to grow up in a world that's safe

without any more war.

                    PRISCILLA
Yep, that'll learn 'em.

                    KERRY-ANNE
Alright, best make tracks. I got shit to do.

                    PRISCILLA
Where are you headed?

                    KERRY-ANNE
North West.

                    PRISCILLA
I'll come for a wander.

They start to wander off.

                    KERRY-ANNE
Ah it's nice to have peace again. God they're weird looking things, people, aren't they?

                    PRISCILLA
The weirdest!

Priscilla jumps up and down in a manic emu tizz.

                    PRISCILLA
Sorry. Excited.

Kerry-Anne and Priscilla exit.

STEVE
What are you gonna do now, Don?

RON
I dunno, little one. Just take it in for a bit I think. Maybe make a list of gratitude. Might meditate.

STEVE
Cool.

Beat.

RON
Kinda want to do it alone, Steve.

STEVE
Oh you want me to go?

RON
Yes.

STEVE
Now?

RON
Yeah, leave me alone.

STEVE
I don't need you anyway, man.

                    RON
Okay, Steve.

                    STEVE
I'm gonna smash you when I get older.

                    RON
No you're not.

                    STEVE
WHATEVER!

           Steve exits.

           Ron takes a moment. Billy enters.
           He yells out in fear.

           He puts his fists up to fight.

                    RON
Bring it on, dickhead.

BLACKOUT

                    THE END

ABOUT THE AUTHOR

XAVIER COY

Xavier Coy is a Sydney based writer and actor. He wrote on season two of Channel 10's acclaimed television series *Five Bedrooms* and has completed a development room for The Full Box's adaptation of their documentary into a drama series, *Opal Cove*.

In 2017 Xavier was awarded the Terracini Estate Residency for writing. Other writing credits include *Not Even God Can Save Us* (ACA), *The World According to Jerry* and *Agency* (KXT Storytellers Festival), *Buried, Are You Listening Now?* and *Distorted* (Old 505 Theatre), *Caught Out* (Sydney Fringe Festival and Bondi Feast) which took out the NIDA Award for Best Writer & winner of Sydney Fringe Award at the 2018 Sydney Fringe Festival, and *Charles & Larry* (Flightpath Theatre).

Recent and exciting news sees *Caught Out* being adapted into a musical format in collaboration with Squabbalogic Independent Musical Theatre Inc. which has been funded by Create NSW and a federal Rise Grant.

Xavier has producing attachments for his feature films, the comedy, *The Dream* (Sugary Rum Productions) and a drama *Changing Tides* (Goose Bridle Productions).

OTHER PLAYS BY XAVIER COY

Fighting
Smokin' Joe
Caught Out
Are You Listening Now?
Distorted
Charles & Larry

COMING SOON

Woyzeck
Not Even God Can Save Us
Together
The Coleslaw Conundrum
The King's Cross
Teamwork
First Christmas
Agency
The World According To Jerry

ORiGiN Theatrical

FOR ALL ENQUIRIES CONTACT: ORiGiN™ Theatrical
PO BOX Q1235, QVB Post Office, Sydney, NSW, 1230, Australia
Phone: (61 2) 8514 5201 | enquiries@originmusic.com.au
www.origintheatrical.com.au
Part of the ORiGiN™ Music Group
An Australian Independent Music Company

www.ingramcontent.com/pod-product-compliance
Lightning Source LLC
Chambersburg PA
CBHW061308110426
42742CB00012BA/2095